大数据科学研究丛书

Structural Equation Modeling in Applied Linguistics in the Era of Big Data

大数据时代应用语言学研究中的结构方程建模

王天剑　王彦之　编著

科 学 出 版 社

北 京

内 容 简 介

传统应用语言学研究主要涉及结构化数据（即小数据）。随着信息技术发展，应用语言学研究也进入了大数据时代。这里的大数据是指应用语言学研究使用的超级语料库，它们具有一般大数据的基本特征。本书属于统计学和语料库语言学交叉学科范畴，着重考察三个方面：①语料库大数据的特征；②常用的语料库分析软件及其在语言数据提取中的应用；③结构方程建模的概念和原理及其利用语料库数据建模的基本方法。

作为一部交叉学科著作，本书可供具有一般英语阅读能力，且对大数据语料库语言学和结构方程建模感兴趣的教师、大学生或科研工作者作为参考性工具书或者教材使用。

图书在版编目（CIP）数据

大数据时代应用语言学研究中的结构方程建模 = Structural Equation Modeling in Applied Linguistics in the Era of Big Data：英文 / 王天剑，王彦之编著. —北京：科学出版社，2019.11

（大数据科学研究丛书）

ISBN 978-7-03-062949-4

Ⅰ. ①大… Ⅱ. ①王… ②王… Ⅲ. ①应用语言学－数据处理－系统建模－研究－英文 Ⅳ. ①H08 ②TP391.92

中国版本图书馆 CIP 数据核字（2019）第 241015 号

责任编辑：马 跃 李 嘉 / 责任校对：杨 赛

责任印制：张 伟 / 封面设计：无极书装

科 学 出 版 社 出版

北京东黄城根北街 16 号

邮政编码：100717

http://www.sciencep.com

北京建宏印刷有限公司 印刷

科学出版社发行 各地新华书店经销

*

2019 年 11 月第 一 版 开本：720 × 1000 B5

2020 年 1 月第二次印刷 印张：11 1/4

字数：226 000

定价：92.00 元

（如有印装质量问题，我社负责调换）

作 者 简 介

王天剑（1968—），汉族，籍贯河南南阳，贵州财经大学外语学院教授，海归博士。近年来在《外语学刊》《外语与外语教学》《中国特殊教育》《中小学英语教学与研究》《中国应用语言学》等刊物上发表论文20余篇，其中2篇被中国人民大学复印资料全文转载；专著《语言焦虑研究入门》（英文，中国社会科学出版社出版）荣获贵州省第十次哲学社会科学奖三等奖。

王彦之（1993—），汉族，籍贯河南南阳，中南大学地球科学与信息物理学院取得硕士学位。近年来在《鲁东大学学报（自然科学版）》《上海工程技术大学学报》《四川理工学院学报（自然科学版）》《水文地质工程地质》等刊物上发表学术论文多篇。

Preface

"Big data" is a label for data sets which are too complex or large to be processed by traditional applications. Challenges range from search and capture to sharing, storage, transfer and analysis. "Big data" is generally related to the employment of predictive analytics or other approaches to extract valuable information from large data sets. It is producing a growing effect on just everything including government, business, science, research, and even our mind.

The book provides clear guidance on how to correctly conduct research using Structural Equation Modeling (SEM) in applied linguistics in the era of big data. The primary purpose is to help new researchers to overcome fears and to encourage them to start the practice of SEM with such data sets.

The book presents SEM in a clear and accessible way for common learners. It focuses on practical methods rather than statistical theories. Even without broad statistical knowledge, readers and applied researchers will find it easy to understand and use SEM with big data. If you are enthusiastic about the technique, you will find the book enlightening.

The book covers various key techniques in SEM with big data, such as the transformation of big data into traditional data, path analysis, factor analysis, structural regression analysis, analysis with order-categorical data, analysis with censored data, data imputation, model comparison and estimation method selection.

The book is organized in line with how readers generally progress with the learning of statistical analysis. General introduction and fundamental concepts are followed by specific techniques; basic techniques are followed by more complex ones.

Simplified examples are provided to illustrate the application of SEM with big data. These examples are mostly adapted from the author's personal research in applied linguistics. Problematic examples are created and included to display the ways to deal with various problems that you may meet in real studies. Plenty of figures and tables are employed to illustrate the steps and procedures of analyses, as well as the output in text or graphic formats. Readers can copy those example data to their own computers and practice the central techniques on their own computers.

The book supports formal course teaching, as well as the self-study of SEM with big data. In any case, you will enjoy the process of learning by doing.

With the inclusion of big data, the book is an update to the similar previous books on SEM. Your knowledge about the vast possibilities of the technique will be greatly expanded. The book can also be applied to the researches in other social and behavioral sciences besides linguistics.

The book is dedicated to the use of Amos, though several other programs are also presently popularly used in SEM, such as EQS, LISREL and Mplus. The use of those programs can be easily grasped once you are familiar with Amos.

Contents

Chapter 1 Introduction

Applied linguistics is a branch of linguistics, which focuses on the teaching and learning of language. Quantitative research in applied linguistics has to take advantage of many statistical techniques, one of which is SEM. In the era of big data, the use of SEM in applied linguistics becomes more complicated. This chapter provides an introduction to the fundamental concepts of the book, the use of big data corpora resources, and SEM with the software Amos. The introduction is supposed to help you understand what is to come in later chapters.

1.1 Applied Linguistics and SEM in Applied Linguistics

1.1.1 Applied Linguistics

Established in the mid 20th century, applied linguistics is an interdisciplinary subject. It is a science concerned with the application of linguistic theories to various fields of studies. It identifies language-relevant problems in real life and attempts to provide solutions to those problems. It is closely related to sociology, anthropology, psychology, communication research, computer science, and education. Pragmatics, discourse analysis, conversation analysis, computer-mediated communication, second language acquisition, sign linguistics and stylistics are all specific branches of applied linguistics.

Applied linguistics first came into being to distinguish itself from general linguistics in the 1950s (Davies & Elder, 2004: 1). Though initiated by experts in Europe, applied linguistics quickly became popular and flourished all over the world. It has always been concerned with language problems, among which is the problem of language teaching and acquisition. In America, Leonard Bloomfield was an early advocator of applying linguistic theories to language teaching. He laid the foundation for the Army Specialized Training Program during World War Ⅱ. Another advocator was Charles Fries, the founder of the English Language Institute at the University of Michigan. In England, the British Association for Applied Linguistics came into being in 1967, and one of its central missions is promoting the study of language teaching and acquisition (Davies & Elder, 2004: 7). Nowadays, language teaching and learning problems have become a global focus of applied linguistics. Narrowly speaking, applied linguistics has been accepted as a professional term for the study of language teaching and acquisition. This book simply follows the trend and adopts such an interpretation of applied linguistics.

Applied linguistics involves many teaching, learning and environmental variables. These variables constitute a complicated hierarchy, affecting the process of language acquisition. Statistical techniques have been widely employed in applied linguistics. To language teachers in China, SEM is a relatively new and challenging statistical method.

1.1.2 SEM in Applied Linguistics

1.1.2.1 Concept of SEM

The term SEM is not coined to refer to a specific technique, but to designate a family of statistical techniques, including correlation, regression, factor analysis, path analysis, structural regression, and so on.

SEM is also called covariance structure analysis, analysis of covariance structures, or causal modeling. But the term "causal" can be misleading. SEM is essentially based on correlation or covariance. When A and B are correlated, you may successfully develop a model in which A is assumed to cause B, but you may as well develop a model in which B is assumed to cause A. So the model cannot decide causal relationships. It can, at most, provide statistical support for a theoretically sound hypothesis.

The origin of SEM dates back to 1904, when Charles Spearman developed the exploratory factor analysis. Later in 1918, Sewall Wright developed path analysis. In 1970s, Karl Gustav Jöreskog et al. combined path analysis and factor analysis into the same statistical system (now called SEM) and developed the computer software LISREL to do the analysis (Kline, 2011: 15). From then on, more and more researchers have improved SEM and developed better software, which has stimulated the widespread use of the technique.

SEM offers researchers an array of methods for examining relationships, testing hypotheses and developing theories. Latent variables can be included in the model to represent underlying factors of observed variables, and measurement errors or influences from unknown variables can be estimated in the analysis (Raykov & Marcoulides, 2006: 7).

1.1.2.2 Uses of SEM in applied linguistics

SEM has long been used in various branches of science. Its use in applied linguistics is relatively new. The following are examples of various relationships studied with SEM. The arrow "→" indicates the direction of prediction or influence.

Pulido and Hambrick (2008: 164) used a sample of 99 adult English-speaking learners of Spanish to examine the relationships among language processing experience, passage sight vocabulary, text comprehension, vocabulary retention, etc. The results from SEM suggested that language processing experience affected passage sight vocabulary which further influenced text comprehension. Text comprehension had an effect on vocabulary retention and growth. The modeling can be summarized as: language experience → sight vocabulary → text comprehension → vocabulary retention and growth.

Guo and Roehrig (2011: 42) investigated the English vocabulary, English syntactic awareness, general reading strategies (meta-cognitive awareness), and English reading comprehension with a sample of 278 adult Chinese EFL learners. The authors used English vocabulary and English syntactic awareness as indicators of the factor L2 knowledge, and reading strategies as the indicator of general reading knowledge. SEM shows that the two factors account for 87% of the variance of reading comprehension, with L2 knowledge being the better predictor of reading comprehension. Multiple groups analysis suggests that the results hold across both the upper and lower groups of readers. The modeling can be summarized as: L2 knowledge + general reading knowledge → reading comprehension.

To examine the respective roles of grammatical and vocabulary knowledge in reading comprehension, Zhang (2012: 558) used a sample of 190 advanced Chinese EFL learners. The result of SEM indicates that reading comprehension is significantly related to vocabulary knowledge, and weakly related to grammatical knowledge. Moreover, implicit grammatical knowledge appears to be more closely related to reading comprehension. The modeling can be summarized as: grammatical knowledge + vocabulary knowledge → reading comprehension.

In a longitudinal study, Netten, Droop and Verhoeven (2011: 413) used 729 L1 and 93 L2 learners of Dutch as participants. Reading comprehension was measured in both grade 4 and grade 6, while language proficiency, decoding, nonverbal reasoning, mathematics, reading motivation, academic self-confidence and home reading resources were all measured in grade 4. SEM is used to analyze the data for L1 and L2 participants separately. The results reveal that, for L1 learners, 60% of the variance of reading comprehension in grade 6 could be directly or indirectly predicted by all the other variables (including the reading comprehension in grade 4). Similar results are obtained for L2 learners. The modeling can be summarized as: proficiency + decoding + reasoning + mathematics + motivation + confidence + resources → reading comprehension.

To test the Simple View of Reading, a theory which suggests that reading comprehension is the product of listening comprehension and word decoding, Verhoeven and Leeuwe (2012: 1805) drew a sample of 1,293 L1 learners and a sample of 394 L2 learners of Dutch. In grades 1, 3 and 5, listening comprehension and word decoding were tested, and in grades 2, 4 and 6, reading comprehension was tested. SEM indicated that reading comprehension could be predicted by listening comprehension and word decoding. In higher grades, the predicting effect of word decoding decreased while that of listening comprehension increased. The relationship and tendency were similar for both L1 and L2 learners, though the relationship between listening comprehension and reading comprehension seemed to be consistently stronger for L1 learners. The modeling can be summarized as: listening + decoding → reading comprehension.

Using SEM, Baker, Stoolmiller, Good III et al. (2011: 331) analyzed the relationships among passage fluency, word reading and reading comprehension. Ninety-six second-graders participated in the study. Those children were simultaneously learning both Spanish and English, with Spanish being the home language (language used at home). The results indicate that comprehension has an influence on passage fluency for both the Spanish and the English languages even when the effect of word fluency is controlled. Though English and Spanish are two languages which differ in orthographic transparency, the relationships appear to be constant across the languages. The modeling can be summarized as: comprehension + word fluency → passage fluency.

Two hundred and twenty-seven non-English-major EFL university students were involved in the study by Wu, Yen and Marek (2011: 118), who investigated the learners' motivation, ability and confidence with questionnaires. Analysis with SEM suggests that confidence can be predicted by motivation and ability. The modeling can be summarized as: motivation + ability → confidence.

1.2 Big Data Corpora and the Extraction of Small Data

In Section 1.1, we focus on the concept of applied linguistics, and the use of SEM in applied linguistics. But the data involved in those SEM studies can all be labeled as small data. Small data are those data which can be directly analyzed by traditional statistical techniques. In this section, we will discuss big data corpora and the extraction of small data from those corpora. The initial letters (or the initial letters of content words) of terms for buttons or options are generally in upper cases. This is applicable to cases throughout this book.

1.2.1 Concept of Big Data

"Big data" is a label for data sets which are too complex or large to be processed by traditional applications. The size of the data sets is so large that commonly used software tools are incapable to capture, manage and process within a tolerable period of time. It requires the integration of a set of techniques and technologies to extract values from datasets which are large and complex.

In a report in 2001, Gartner Group's (then Meta Group) analyst Doug Laney put forward the 3-dimensional data growth features: increasing variety, volume, and velocity (Laney, 2001). In 2012, Laney further defined big data as high-volume, high-variety and/or high-velocity information assets which need new forms of processing to promote discovery, decision making and process optimization (Laney, 2012). Currently, it is universally agreed that by means of specific technology and approach, we can extract valuable information from big data. Moreover, some experts have added new dimensions (such as "veracity" "variability") to better define the concept of big data. But anyway, it is the size which determines whether the data sets can be labeled as big data or not. Big data may include structured, unstructured or semi-structured data. To enhance the generating and processing of big data, Google Company put forward a program model called MapReduce in 2004. It has a parallel algorithm working on a cluster of loosely or tightly connected computer clusters. The program model is made up of two parts: the Map part and the Reduce part. The Map part does the filtering and classifying task, while the Reduce part does the summarizing task. The former sorts items into groups, and the latter gives a summary to the items in each group (counting the number or frequency). The MapReduce system coordinates the computer clusters in the processing of the data. The program model is so successful that its algorithm is replicated by others. In 2011, Apache Software Foundation developed an open-source software called Apache Hadoop which incorporates the functions of MapReduce. Apache Hadoop is composed of two parts: one for storing data (Hadoop Distributed File System), and the other for processing data (MapReduce). It supports the parallel processing of big data across computer clusters, and is widely used by organizations and companies for production and study.

1.2.2 Big Data Corpora

1.2.2.1 Features of corpora

In applied linguistics research, the frequently used big data sets are corpora. A corpus is a set of text, audio, or video files (called text corpus, audio corpus and video corpus respectively). If two or three of the media are involved in a data set, it is called a multimedia corpus. Presently, techniques for coping with text corpora are well developed. In this book, the term "corpus" is to be accepted as text corpora, unless otherwise specified.

A corpus is qualified to be called big data, because it has most of the defining features of big data.

Firstly, it has a high volume. In terms of size, a corpus is large enough to be called big data. For example, the American National Corpus (ANC) has 40-50 million words. The British National Corpus (BNC) contains 100 million words.

Secondly, a corpus has a high variety of big data. A balanced corpus covers texts of all genres, and the variety is high enough to be called big data. For example, ANC includes data from court transcript, email, debate transcript, essay, government document, fiction, non-fiction, journal, newspaper, letter, spoken language, technology, travel guide, twitter, joke, blog, script, ficlet, movie spam, and other texts. BNC has similar coverage.

Thirdly, a corpus has high veracity of big data. The texts covered by a corpus are all from real life.

1.2.2.2 Wide acceptance of corpora as big data

In fact, many organizations and experts have accepted corpora as big data sets. For example, from the database of Springer Link, ScienceDirect, ProQuest, etc., if we search for "'big data' AND corpus", many records can be found (Figure 1.1-Figure 1.3).

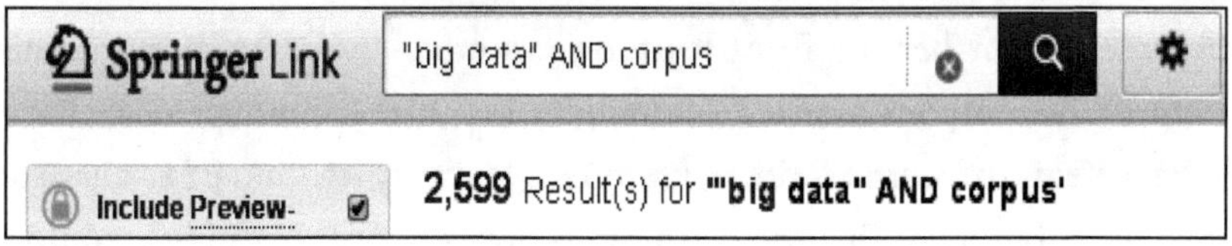

Figure 1.1 Results from searching for "'big data' AND corpus" in Springer Link

Source: Retrieved from the library database of Central South University, China [2019-05-08]

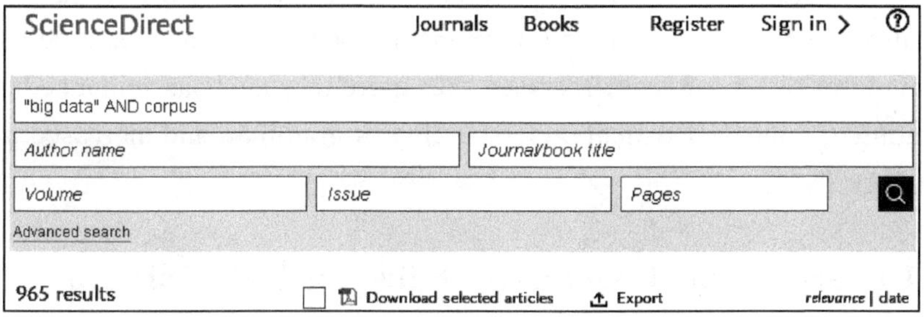

Figure 1.2 Results from searching for "'big data' AND corpus" in ScienceDirect

Source: Retrieved from the library database of Central South University, China [2019-05-08]

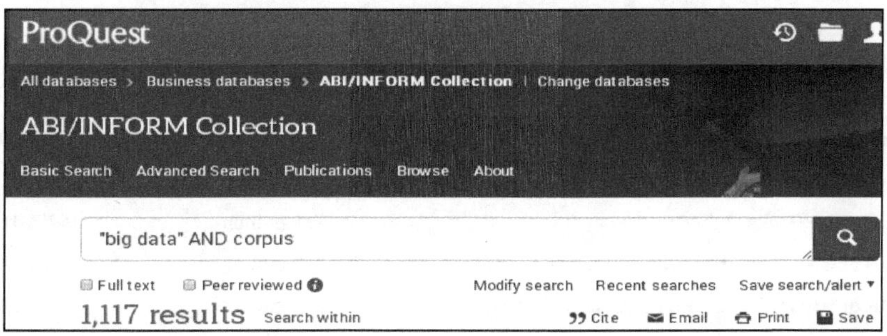

Figure 1.3 Results from searching for "'big data' AND corpus" in ProQuest

Source: Retrieved from the library database of Central South University, China [2019-05-08]

In a word, corpora have been gradually accepted as big data. In this book, we may use "corpora" or "big data corpora" alternatively. In recent years, more and more corpora have been created for linguistic researches. Some of the corpora are available online, and others can be used offline. Corresponding sorts of software have been developed to help researchers to extract valuable information from corpora.

Nowadays, many experts are using corpora in applied linguistic researches. Phoocharoensil (2012: 507) investigated Thai EFL students' attitudes to learning grammar through concordance lines (extracted from corpora). The author discovered that most students can benefit from learning grammar by using corpora, and have a positive attitude to corpora-assisted learning. Lin (2016) conducted a case study to examine the effects of corpus-aided grammar learning in the EFL classroom. The results revealed that data-driven learning (corpus-aided learning) could enhance college students' learning attitudes in general. Furthermore, data-driven learning is considered to be innovative and interesting by the early-career teachers involved in the study. Liu and Jiang (2009: 61) explored the effects of integrating corpus and contextualized lexicogrammar in both foreign and second language learning situations. They found several positive effects of the approach, such as enhanced grasp of lexicogrammar, improved critical understanding of grammar, and increased discovery of learning skills.

1.2.3 Extracting Small Data from Online Big Data Corpora

There are presently many online corpora. Here is a list of some of the most famous ones (Table 1.1).

Table 1.1 Famous online corpora

Corpus names	Words	Time periods
Global Web-based English (GloWbE)	1.9 billion	2012-2013
Hansard Corpus	1.6 billion	1803-2005
Early English Books Online	755 million	1470s-1690s
Corpus of Contemporary American English (COCA)	560 million	1990-2017
Corpus of Historical American English (COHA)	400 million	1810-2009
Corpus of US Supreme Court Opinions	130 million	1790s-present (2017)
TIME Magazine Corpus	100 million	1923-2006
Corpus of American Soap Operas	100 million	2001-2012
British National Corpus (BNC)	100 million	1980s-1993

Source: https://www.english-corpora.org/corpora.asp?b=y[2019-05-08]. Corpus of US Supreme Court Opinions is a dynamic corpus and was last updated in 2017

An online big data corpus may contain millions of or hundreds of millions of words (tokens). In applied linguistics research, it is not possible to analyze the data directly with SEM. But we can extract small data from big data, or extract data which can be analyzed directly with SEM. Section 1.2.3.1 to Section 1.2.3.3 focus on the means of extracting small data from BNC (https://www.english-corpora.org/bnc/).

1.2.3.1 Searching for the frequency of isolated words or symbols

Frequency is the information which can be easily extracted and used in the study of applied linguistics. To search for the frequency, we can employ a range of methods, such as the wildcard, specific symbol and part of speech. When the part of speech is used, we have to be familiar with the correspondence between symbols and meanings (Table 1.2). In this section, we focus on the frequency of isolated words and symbols.

Table 1.2 Part of speech for searching

Variants of symbols				Meanings
[nn*]	NOUN	N	_nn	Common nouns
[np*]	NAME	NP	_np	Proper nouns
[n*]	NOUN+	N+	_n	Common and proper nouns
[vv*]	VERB	V	_vv	Lexical verbs (no do, be, have)
[v*]	VERB+	V+	_v	All verbs (including do, be, have)
[j*]	ADJ	J	_j	Adjectives
[r*]	ADV	R	_r	Adverbs
[p*]	PRON		_p	Pronouns
[i*]	PREP		_i	Prepositions
[a*]	ART		_a	Articles
[d*]	DET		_d	Determiners
[c*]	CONJ		_c	Conjunctions
[x*]	NEG		_x	Negation
[m*]	NUM		_m	Numbers

Source: https://www.english-corpora.org/bnc/[2019-05-08]

Note: In BNC, the web address for any searching result is always https://www.english-corpora.org/bnc/

A. Simple searching for the distribution

If we search for the word "the" in BNC, we can type it into the search query area (Figure 1.4), and click "Find matching strings". The result will show the frequency of the word "the" in the whole corpus.

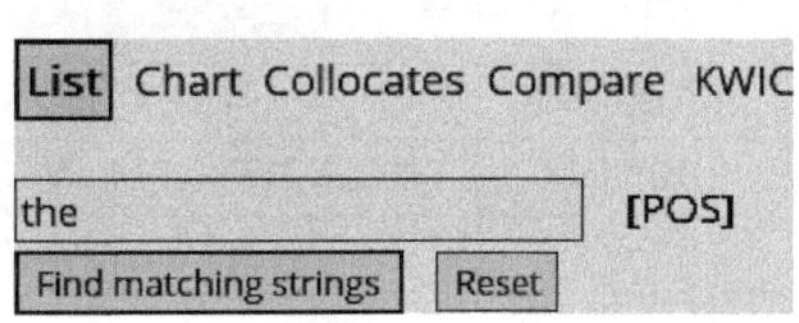

Figure 1.4 Typing "the" into the search query area

Source: https://www.english-corpora.org/bnc/[2019-05-08]

On the home page for searching, if we click "Sections and Chart", we can discover the frequency of the target word in a specific domain covered by the corpus (Figure 1.5). The word "the" appears 409,013 times in spoken English, 834,722 times in fictions, 427,243 times in magazines, 635,001 times in newspapers, 1,136,961 times in non-academic writings,

1,128,125 times in academic works, and 1,400,734 times in miscellaneous writings. We can compare the frequencies in different genres. People tend to use "the" most frequently in academic English (73,581.36 times in per million running words), and least frequently in spoken English (41,050.47 times in every million running words).

SECTION	ALL	SPOKEN	FICTION	MAGAZINE	NEWSP-APER	NON-ACAD	ACAD-EMIC	MISC
FREQ	5971799	409013	834722	427243	635001	1136961	1128125	1400734
WORDS(M)	100	10.0	15.9	7.3	10.5	16.5	15.3	20.8
PER MIL	59,717.99	41,050.47	52,467.51	58,832.77	60,670.30	68,926.84	73,581.36	67,229.34
SEE ALL SUB-SECTIONS AT ONCE								

Figure 1.5 Frequency of "the" in different genres of English

Source: https://www.english-corpora.org/bnc/[2019-05-08]

B. Searching with the wildcard "*" following a word

The "*" can stand for a punctuation mark, a symbol, or a cluster of letters (word or part of a word). If we search for the "the *", we can see the frequency of any word, symbol or punctuation mark immediately following "the" (Figure 1.6).

1	THE FIRST	60308	
2	THE SAME	57466	
3	THE OTHER	39622	
4	THE MOST	32962	
5	THE NEW	29680	
6	THE'	29152	
7	THE END	27180	
8	THE WORLD	27018	
9	THE TIME	26713	
10	THE WAY	25096	

Figure 1.6 Frequency of words, punctuations and symbols following "the"

Source: https://www.english-corpora.org/bnc/[2019-05-08]

C. Searching for a word containing the wildcard "*"

If we search for "dis*ly", we can get the frequency of any word beginning with "dis" and ending with "ly" (Figure 1.7).

DISTINCTLY	783
DISCREETLY	306
DISPROPORTIONATELY	235
DISORDERLY	202
DISMISSIVELY	144
DISTANTLY	143
DISTINCTIVELY	129
DISHONESTLY	109
DISASTROUSLY	106
DISTURBINGLY	101

Figure 1.7 Frequency of "dis*ly"

Source: https://www.english-corpora.org/bnc/[2019-05-08]

D. Searching for a word containing the symbol "?"

The symbol "?" can only stand for a single letter. If you search for "dis?n*", you may get any word with one letter between "dis" and "n", and one or more letters following "n" (Figure 1.8).

DISINTEGRATION	309
DISINTERESTED	170
DISINTEGRATED	148
DISENCHANTMENT	138
DISINFECTANT	134
DISINCENTIVE	129
DISINTEGRATING	110
DISINFECTION	103
DISENTANGLE	103
DISINTEGRATE	98

Figure 1.8 Frequency of "dis?n*"

Source: https://www.english-corpora.org/bnc/[2019-05-08]

E. Searching for a lemma

Search for the lemma of a word (using "[lemma]" or the uppercase of a lemma), you can get the total frequency of various forms of the same word. For example, if you search for "[sleep]" or "SLEEP", you will get the following result (Figure 1.9).

SLEEP	7139
SLEPT	1623
SLEEPING	1051
SLEEPS	241
SLEEP.	1

Figure 1.9 Frequency of "[sleep]*"

Source: https://www.english-corpora.org/bnc/[2019-05-08]

Note: In BNC, "SLEEP." appears once in the sentence "She will drift into sleep., ...", as can be seen by clicking on the word. This strange form seems to be a mistake

F. Searching for a word of a particular part of speech

To limit the part of speech of a word to be searched, you can attach a part of speech. For example, to search for "LIE_v" or "[lie]_v", you can find the uses of "lie" as a verb (Figure 1.10).

LYING	4289
LIE	4067
LIES	3915
LIED	547
LAIN	305

Figure 1.10 Frequency of "LIE_v"

Source: https://www.english-corpora.org/bnc/[2019-05-08]

G. Searching for alternative words

You can use alternants in a search. The alternative words need to be separated by "|". For example, if you search for "will|can|may|must|shall", you will get the frequencies of all those words (Figure 1.11).

WILL	248439
CAN	229823
MAY	125565
MUST	69514
SHALL	19407

Figure 1.11 Frequency of "will|can|may|must|shall"

Source: https://www.english-corpora.org/bnc/[2019-05-08]

H. Searching for synonyms with "=word"

You can get synonyms of a word by searching for "=word". For example, if you search for "=big", you will get the frequencies of all the synonyms of "big" (Figure 1.12).

GOOD[S]	79878
GREAT[S]	46108
IMPORTANT[S]	38450
HIGH[S]	37700
LARGE[S]	33965
BIG[S]	24382
SIGNIFICANT[S]	11914
WIDE[S]	11735
DEEP[S]	10141
CONSIDERABLE[S]	9412

Figure 1.12 Frequency of "=big"

Source: https://www.english-corpora.org/bnc/[2019-05-08]

I. Searching for synonyms with "=lemma"

If we use the lemma in searching for synonyms, we will get synonyms in different forms. For example, if we search for "=HAPPY" (only upper cases can be recognized), we will get the following result (Figure 1.13).

HAPPY[S]	11166
CONTENT[S]	5946
PLEASED[S]	4037
LUCKY[S]	3872
GLAD[S]	3730
CONTENTS[S]	2876
DELIGHTED[S]	2181
FORTUNATE[S]	1259
CHEERFUL[S]	1074
HAPPIER[S]	872

Figure 1.13 Frequency of "=HAPPY"

Source: https://www.english-corpora.org/bnc/[2019-05-08]

1.2.3.2 Searching for the frequency and context of a string of words or collocates

In second language learning, we may want to know whether a string of words or collocates is acceptable or popularly used. In such cases, we can search for the strings in a corpus.

A. Searching for a string with a wildcard

We can not only search for the frequency of a specified string, but also a string with a wildcard. For example, searching for "more * than", we can obtain a string with any one word between them (Figure 1.14).

MORE IMPORTANT THAN	655
MORE OFTEN THAN	433
MORE SO THAN	239
MORE EXPENSIVE THAN	193
MORE LIKELY THAN	189
MORE COMPLEX THAN	156
MORE DIFFICULT THAN	154
MORE EFFECTIVE THAN	143
MORE POWERFUL THAN	135
MORE QUICKLY THAN	131

Figure 1.14 Frequency of "more * than"

Source: https://www.english-corpora.org/bnc/[2019-05-08]

B. Searching for a string with the inclusion of part of speech

You can limit the part of speech of a word in a string. For example, searching "black [n*]" or "black NOUN", we can get all the frequencies of "black + noun" (Figure 1.15).

BLACK HOLE	532
BLACK PEOPLE	478
BLACK HAIR	466
BLACK HOLES	257
BLACK SEA	250
BLACK EYES	204
BLACK WOMEN	191
BLACK MAN	165
BLACK PEPPER	165
BLACK MARKET	157

Figure 1.15 Frequency of "black NOUN"

Source: https://www.english-corpora.org/bnc/[2019-05-08]

C. Searching for a string with the exclusion of part of speech

It is also possible to exclude words of a specific part of speech from a string. For example, if you search for "pretty –NOUN" (a space and a minus symbol exist between the two parts), you will get strings in which the word directly following "pretty" is not a noun (Figure 1.16).

PRETTY GOOD	476
PRETTY WELL	386
PRETTY,	309
PRETTY MUCH	293
PRETTY.	193
PRETTY SURE	160
PPETTY LITTLE	118
PRETTY AND	101

Figure 1.16 Frequency of "pretty –NOUN"

Source: https://www.english-corpora.org/bnc/[2019-05-08]

D. Searching for a string with a combination of specifications

We can also combine the different kinds of searches to create fairly complex phrases. For example, to search for "fast|slow|quick NOUN", you will get "fast NOUN" "slow NOUN" "quick NOUN" (Figure 1.17).

QUICK LOOK	156
FAST FOOD	154
QUICK GLANCE	131
FAST BOWLER	130
SLOW MOTION	105
QUICK SUCCESSION	95
SLOW PROGRESS	92
SLOW MOVEMENT	78
SLOW PROCESS	69
FAST LANE	65

Figure 1.17 Frequency of "fast|slow|quick NOUN "

Source: https://www.english-corpora.org/bnc/[2019-05-08]

E. Searching for keywords in specific contexts

We can discover the patterns in which a word occurs, by sorting the words to the left and/or the right. For example, we can find out which word is most frequently used immediately (1 word) to the left of "problem" when it is a noun. What we have to do is to click "KWIC" (Keyword in Context), type "problem_n" into the query area, and specify the demand (position) by clicking the corresponding cell below the query area (Figure 1.18).

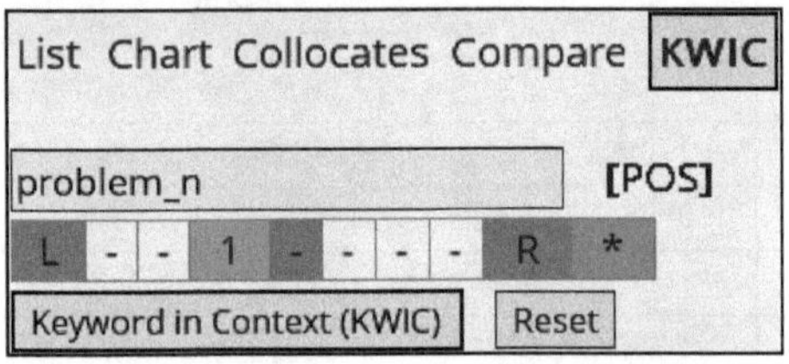

Figure 1.18 Searching for the word to the left of "problem_n"

Source: https://www.english-corpora.org/bnc/[2019-05-08]

The results suggest that "a" is the word which appears most frequently preceding "problem" when it is used as a noun (Figure 1.19).

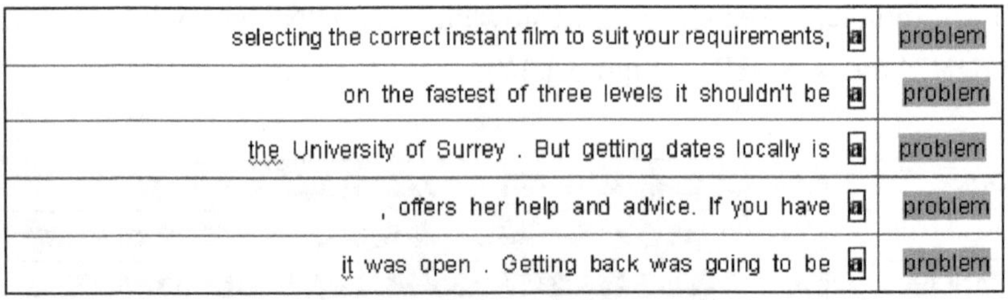

Figure 1.19 Results for searching for the word to the left of "problem_n"

Source: https://www.english-corpora.org/bnc/[2019-05-08]

F. Searching for collocates with a limitation of part of speech

If we are interested in collocates (disconnected units), it is also possible to find out relevant information. For example, we can select "Collocates" and search for the collocation between "happy" and "NOUN" in which the "NOUN" is within the space of 4 words following "happy" (Figure 1.20).

The results reveal that "birthday" is the word most frequently used within the space of 4 words following "happy", with "life" coming next in frequency (Figure 1.21).

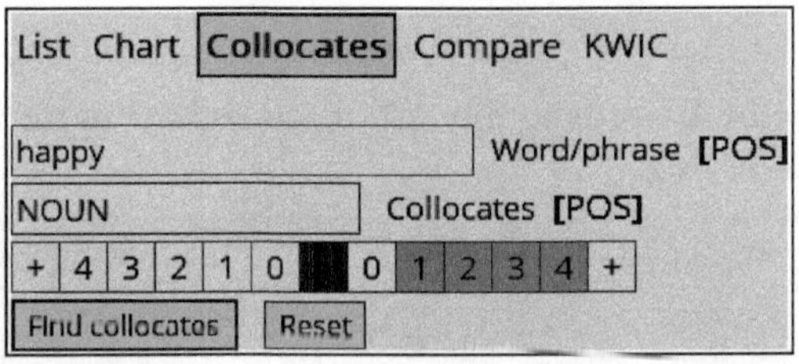

Figure 1.20 Searching for collocates with a noun to the right of "happy"

Source: https://www.english-corpora.org/bnc/[2019-05-08]

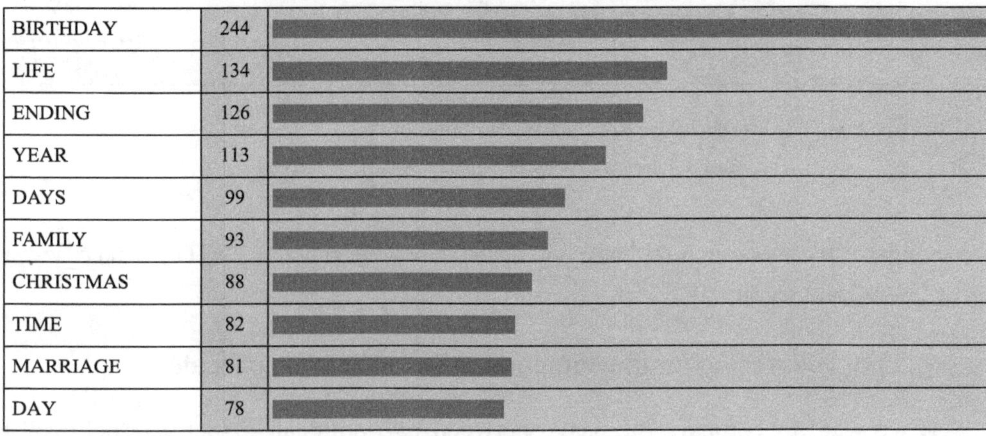

Figure 1.21 Results for the collocates of "happy" and "NOUN"

Source: https://www.english-corpora.org/bnc/[2019-05-08]

G. Searching for collocates with several specifications

For both the "Word/phrase" and "Collocates" fields, we can include the full range of searches, such as words, substrings, parts of speech, lemmas and synonyms. For example, we can search for "face_vv" (in the "Word/phrase" field) + "*" (any word) (in the "Collocates" field) (Figure 1.22).

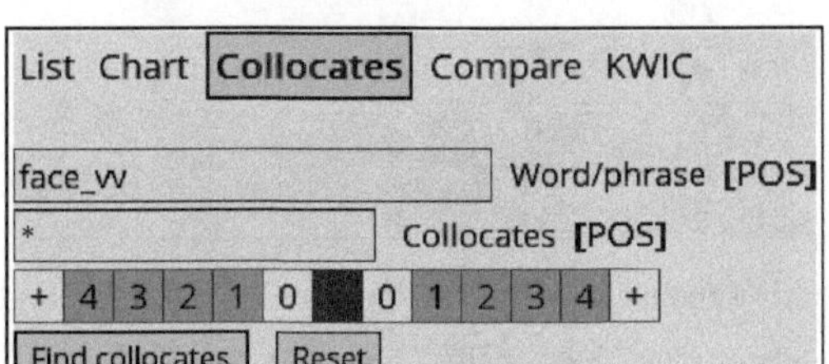

Figure 1.22 Full range search for the collocates of "face_vv" + "*"

Source: https://www.english-corpora.org/bnc/[2019-05-08]

The results suggest that "to" is the word most frequently collocated with the verb "face" within the space of 4 words to the left or the right (Figure 1.23).

TO	2969
THE	2706
AND	1214
A	923
OF	890
IN	705
IT	608

Figure 1.23 Results for searching for "face_vv" + "*"

Source: https://www.english-corpora.org/bnc/[2019-05-08]

Similarly, we can search for "face_vv" + "NOUN", "face_vv" + "WITH", "face_vv" + "=difficulty" and so on.

1.2.3.3 Searching for the comparison between two collocates

If we want to compare the usage between two collocates, such as "believe" + "NOUN" and "trust" + "NOUN", we can click "Compare", place the words to be compared in the "Word1" and "Word2" field, enter the shared collocate(s) in the "Collocates" field, and specify the range within which the shared collocate(s) may occur (Figure 1.24).

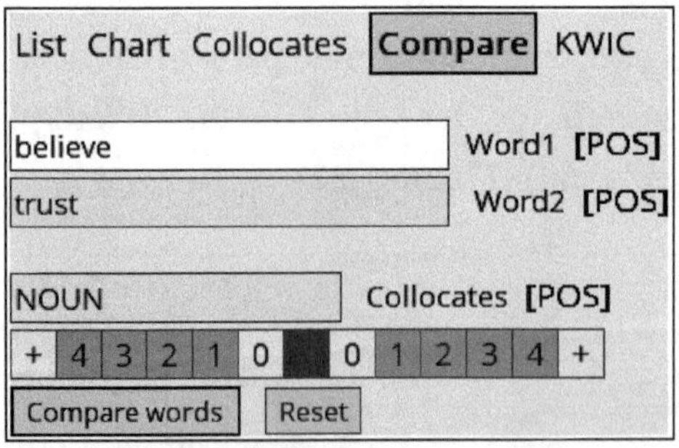

Figure 1.24 Comparing the usage between "believe" + "NOUN" and "trust" + "NOUN"

Source: https://www.english-corpora.org/bnc/[2019-05-08]

The results are shown in Figure 1.25. The number following a compared word is the frequency ratio of that word to the other word in the specified collocations. Here 2.04 suggests that there are 2.04 tokens of "believe" (WORD 1) for every token of "trust" (WORD 2); 0.49 suggests that there are 0.49 tokens of "trust" for every token of "believe". W1 and W2 are the frequencies of WORD 1 and WORD 2 collocating with the preceding word. The W1/W2 means dividing W1 by W2. If W2 is zero, it is replaced by 0.50. The SCORE for WORD 1 is calculated by dividing W1 by W2 with the frequency ratio of WORD 1, and the SCORE for WORD 2 is calculated by dividing W2 by W1 with the frequency ratio of WORD 2. In the example, the results show that 1) "believe" is more frequently used with a noun than "trust", with a ratio of 2.04 to 1, and 2) "believe" is strongly collocated with "scientists" "Christians", etc., while "trust" is strongly collocated with "deed" "gardens", etc.

WORD 1 (W1): **BELIEVE** (2.04)					
	WORD	W1	W2	W1/W2	SCORE
1	SCIENTISTS	62	0	124.0	60.9
2	CHRISTIANS	58	0	116.0	56.9
3	DETECTIVES	45	0	90.0	44.2
4	ANALYSTS	43	0	86.0	42.2
5	OBSERVERS	35	0	70.0	34.4
6	VIOLENCE	22	0	44.0	21.6
7	GHOSTS	21	0	42.0	20.6
8	AGE	20	0	40.0	19.6
9	CRITICS	18	0	36.0	17.7
10	ECONOMISTS	18	0	36.0	17.7

WORD 2 (W2): **TRUST** (0.49)					
	WORD	W2	W1	W2/W1	SCORE
1	DEED	55	0	110.0	224.2
2	GARDENS	49	0	98.0	199.7
3	BENEFICIARY	48	0	96.0	195.6
4	CHARITY	41	0	82.0	167.1
5	ASSETS	39	0	78.0	158.9
6	WILDFOWL	39	0	78.0	158.9
7	CHILDBIRTH	30	0	60.0	122.3
8	BREACH	58	1	58.0	118.2
9	CORPORATION	28	0	56.0	114.1
10	BENEFICIARIES	26	0	52.0	106.0

Figure 1.25 The difference between "believe" + "NOUN" and "trust" + "NOUN"

Source: https://www.english-corpora.org/bnc/[2019-05-08]

1.2.4 Extracting Small Data From Offline Big Data Corpora

We can download big data from the online corpora, or develop our own big data corpora. These corpora can be put under an umbrella term: offline big data corpora. We can extract useful information from offline big data corpora with the help of corpus analysis tools. There are various tools, such as WordSmith Tools, AntConc, Range, Readability Analyzer, Lexical Complexity Analyzer and Syntactic Complexity Analyzer. The following are examples of extracting small data from offline corpora developed by the author.

1.2.4.1 WordSmith Tools

WordSmith Tools was first developed by Mike Scott in 1996. It is an integrated software for examining how words behave in texts. We can use the tools to find out how words are used in our own texts, or in those of others. The software can provide a list of all the words or word-clusters used in a text, set out in frequency or the alphabetical order. You also have a chance to see any word or phrase in a specific context, so that you can find out what sort of company it keeps. The keywords in a text can also be revealed. Here the searching for the frequency list and the calculation of the statistics of a text are to be illustrated.

A. Searching for the frequency list

To search for the frequency list of words, we have to 1) run the software, 2) click "WordList", 3) click "Choose Text Now", 4) select the text(s), 5) close the interface, and 6) click "Make a wordlist now". The results will be displayed. Here is a list of word frequencies calculated from a corpus by the author (Figure 1.26). The results suggest that "the" occurs 19,175 times in the corpus, which accounts for 5.93% of the total words. It appears in 93 texts. "100%" means that "the" occurs in all the texts.

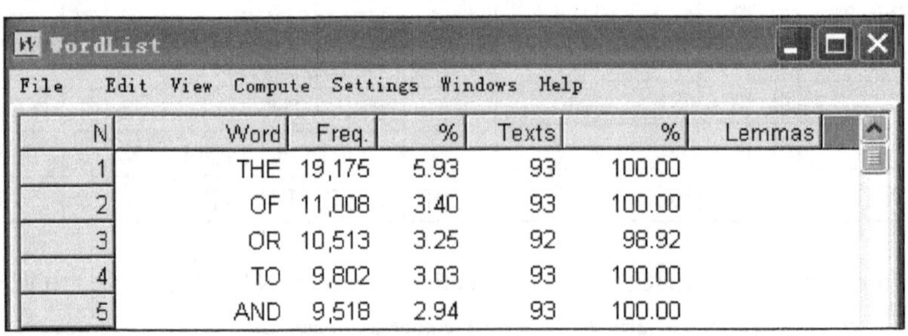
WordList

File Edit View Compute Settings Windows Help

N	Word	Freq.	%	Texts	%	Lemmas
1	THE	19,175	5.93	93	100.00	
2	OF	11,008	3.40	93	100.00	
3	OR	10,513	3.25	92	98.92	
4	TO	9,802	3.03	93	100.00	
5	AND	9,518	2.94	93	100.00	

Figure 1.26 Word frequency by the WordList of WordSmith Tools

B. Searching for statistics of a text

With WordSmith Tools, we can get various statistics, such as the number of types or tokens, the type/token ratio, the mean word length and the mean sentence length. What we have to do is to 1) run the software, 2) make a word list, and 3) select "Statistics" from the menu. The information will be displayed immediately following the procedure. Figure 1.27 shows the statistics of a corpus by the author. The first column ("N") displays the names of the variables, the second column ("Overall") gives the values of the variables based on the total corpus, and the following columns give the values of the variables based on individual files.

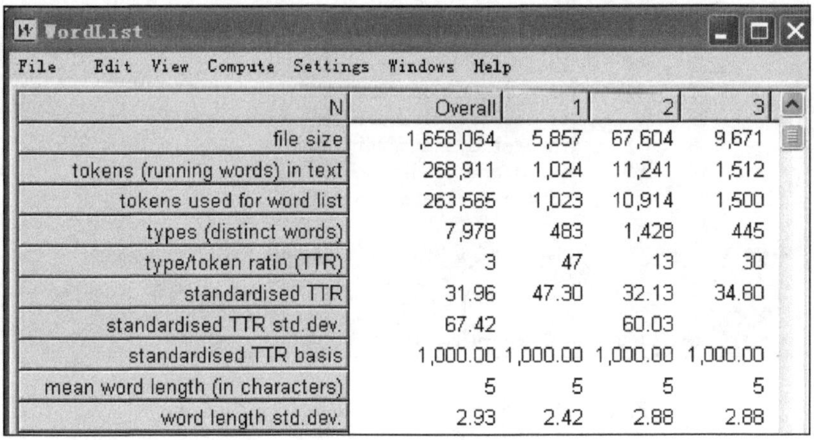

WordList

File Edit View Compute Settings Windows Help

N	Overall	1	2	3
file size	1,658,064	5,857	67,604	9,671
tokens (running words) in text	268,911	1,024	11,241	1,512
tokens used for word list	263,565	1,023	10,914	1,500
types (distinct words)	7,978	483	1,428	445
type/token ratio (TTR)	3	47	13	30
standardised TTR	31.96	47.30	32.13	34.80
standardised TTR std.dev.	67.42		60.03	
standardised TTR basis	1,000.00	1,000.00	1,000.00	1,000.00
mean word length (in characters)	5	5	5	5
word length std.dev.	2.93	2.42	2.88	2.88

Figure 1.27 Statistics by the WordList of WordSmith Tools

1.2.4.2 AntConc

AntConc was first developed by Laurence Anthony in 2002. It is a versatile tool for anyone who is interested in obtaining word, N-gram unit, and keyword frequency analyses from a corpus. Frequency analysis results can also be used for understanding other features of a text or corpus. The searching for N-grams and word counts needed for calculating the information density are illustrated here.

A. Searching for the N-grams

To find out the chunks with AntConc, we may begin with the searching for the N-grams in a corpus. What we have to do is to 1) click the "Clusters/N-Grams", 2) set the "N-Gram Size" (the minimum and maximum numbers of words), 3) set the "Min. Freq." (the minimum frequency), 4) set the "Min. Range" (the minimum number of files in which the chunk occurs), and 5) run the analysis. Take the searching for the chunks in a corpus of 100 software licenses for example. The author is interested in chunks with the size of 4-5 words, a frequency of no less than 10, and a range of no less than 5. The results suggest that the most frequently used chunk is "the terms of this", which appears 264 times in 76 of the 100 files in the corpus (Figure 1.28).

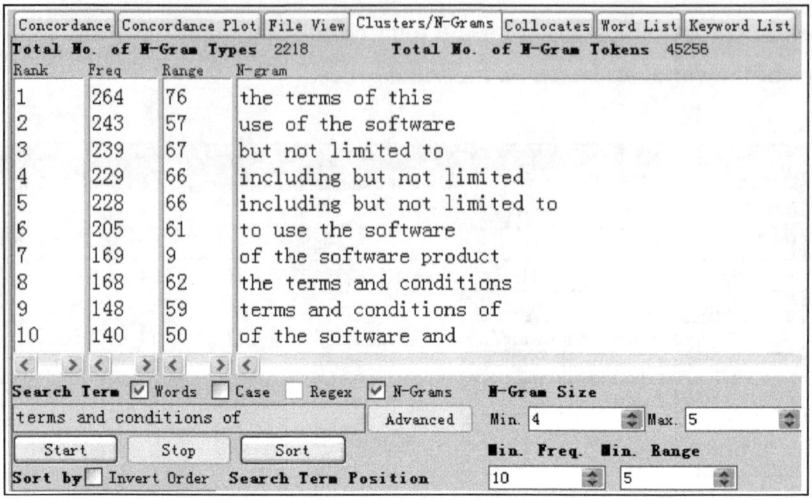

Figure 1.28 Searching for chunks with AntConc

B. Searching for word counts needed for calculating the information density

AntConc can be used to calculate the information density of a text file or a corpus. Information density refers to the proportion of content words in a file or a collection of files. Content words are nouns, verbs, adjectives, adverbs and cardinal numerals. To compute the content words, we have to employ the software tree tagger, go tagger, claws, etc., to tag the part of speech as follows.

> Workday_NN provides_VVZ unified_JJ finance_NN,_, human_JJ resources_NNS and_CC student/faculty_NN lifecycle_NN management_NN cloud_NN applications_NNS designed_VVN for_IN the_DT way_NN people_NNS work_VVP in_IN today's_JJ organisations_NNS._SENT…

When the file is tagged, we can run AntConc to sort and calculate the content words, and compute the information density. To perform the searching, we have to 1) click the "Concordance" (for listing the lines with the object), 2) click the "Regex" (regulation expression, such as "_NN" for nouns and, "VV" for verbs), 3) enter the regulation expression, and 4) run the searching. The "Concordance Hits" will indicate the total number of the target terms found. For example, in the searching shown in Figure 1.29, "Concordance Hits" is 763, which suggests that 763 target terms (nouns) are found in the corpus involved.

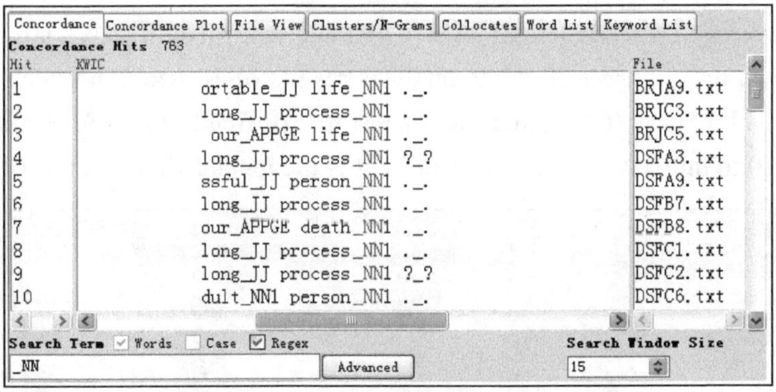

Figure 1.29 Searching for nouns with AntConc

1.2.4.3 Range

Range was developed by Batia Laufer and Paul Nation in 1995 (originally called Lexical Frequency Profile). It can be used to compare the vocabulary of up to 32 different texts at the same time. For each word in the files, it can provide a distribution figure (how many texts the word appears in). With three base lists of words (BASEWRD1 includes the most frequently used 1,000 word families, BASEWRD2 includes the less frequently used 1,000 word families, and BASEWRD3 covers 570 academic word families beyond BASEWRD1 and BASEWRD2), it can show the distribution of the words in the corpus. Table 1.3 shows the results of an analysis. The first column indicates the categories, and the second, third and fourth columns show the tokens, types and families belonging to each category (and the percentages).

Table 1.3 Analysis results from Range

Word lists	Tokens/Percentages (%)	Types/Percentages (%)	Families
One	48,995/68.35	1,243/31.09	614
Two	3,138/4.38	322/8.05	176
Three	8,427/11.75	822/20.56	378
Not in the list	11,127/15.52	1,611/40.30	?????
Total	71,687/100	3,998/100	1,168

Note: A total of 1,611 types do not belong to the three categories covered by the word list. The "?????" is used because the software can not calculate the corresponding families.

1.2.4.4 Readability Analyzer

Readability Analyzer is a software written by Xu Jiajin and Jia Yunlong in 2009. It is a tool designed to extract basic readability statistics from English texts. It can compute the Flesch Reading Ease and Flesch-Kincaid Grade Level, as well as the number of sentences, average sentence length (ASL), average word length (AWL), the number of tokens, and so on. Figure 1.30 is the analysis results of 10 texts, in which “txt09” has the lowest reading ease (6.70), and the highest text difficulty (93.30), requiring a grade level of 22.10 to understand. In other words, it is the most difficult in the 10 texts.

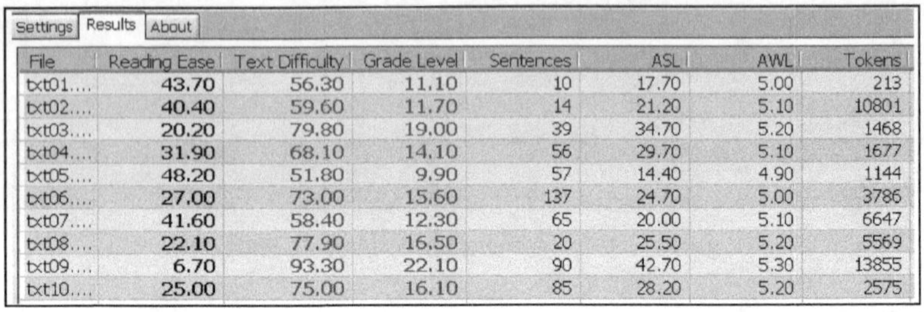

File	Reading Ease	Text Difficulty	Grade Level	Sentences	ASL	AWL	Tokens
txt01....	43.70	56.30	11.10	10	17.70	5.00	213
txt02....	40.40	59.60	11.70	14	21.20	5.10	10801
txt03....	20.20	79.80	19.00	39	34.70	5.20	1468
txt04....	31.90	68.10	14.10	56	29.70	5.10	1677
txt05....	48.20	51.80	9.90	57	14.40	4.90	1144
txt06....	27.00	73.00	15.60	137	24.70	5.00	3786
txt07....	41.60	58.40	12.30	65	20.00	5.10	6647
txt08....	22.10	77.90	16.50	20	25.50	5.20	5569
txt09....	6.70	93.30	22.10	90	42.70	5.30	13855
txt10....	25.00	75.00	16.10	85	28.20	5.20	2575

Figure 1.30 Analysis results from Readability Analyzer

1.2.4.5 Lexical Complexity Analyzer and Syntactic Complexity Analyzer

Lexical Complexity Analyzer (Lu, 2012: 190) and Syntactic Complexity Analyzer (Lu, 2011: 36; Lu & Ai, 2015: 16-17) are used to analyze the lexical complexity and syntactic complexity. All input files must be part-of-speech-tagged and lemmatized first, and should contain a minimum of 50 words. The online version is also available at http://aihaiyang.com/software/lca/single/.

To use the online version of Lexical Complexity Analyzer, you have to enter the text, select the measures, and run the software. The results include LD (lexical density), LS1 (lexical sophistication-I), LS2 (lexical sophistication-II), VS1 (verbal sophistication-I), VS2 (verbal sophistication-II), CVS1 (corrected VSI), NDW (number of different words), NDWZ (first 50 words), NDWERZ (expected random 50), NDWESZ (expected sequence 50), TTR (type-token ratio), MSTTR (mean segmental TTR), CTTR (corrected TTR), RTTR (root TTR), LOGTTR (bilogarithmic TTR), UBER (Uber index), VV1 (verb variation), SVV1 (squared VVI), CVV1 (corrected VVI), LV (lexical word variation), VV2 (verb variation II), NV (noun variation), ADJV (adjective variation), ADVV (adverb variation) and MODV (modifier variation). Table 1.4 displays the selected results of two short texts (Text 1 and Text 2) analyzed with Lexical Complexity Analyzer. As is clear, the words in “Text 2” are more complex than those in “Text 1” for 6 of the 10 indexes.

Table 1.4 Selected results from Lexical Complexity Analyzer

Texts	LD	LS1	LS2	VS1	VS2	CVS1	NDW	NDWZ	NDWERZ	NDWESZ
Text 1	0.47	0.21	0.21	0.17	0.33	0.41	43	37	37.00	38.10
Text 2	0.52	0.53	0.42	0.50	3.00	1.22	43	35	33.20	35.10

Syntactic Complexity Analyzer is designed to automate syntactic complexity analysis using 14 different measures. We can use the software online (https://aihaiyang.com/software/l2sca/single/). The steps are similar to those for running the Lexical Complexity Analyzer. The results include W (word count), S (sentence), VP (verb phrase), C (clause), T (T-unit), DC (dependent clause), CT (complex T-unit), CP (coordinate phrase), CN (complex normal), MLS (mean length of sentence), MLT (mean length of T-unit), etc.

1.3 Amos and Its Uses in SEM

Amos stands for analysis of moment structures. It is one of the popular programs used in SEM. Amos employs maximum likelihood (ML), scale-free least squares, unweighted least squares (ULS), generalized least squares (GLS), and Browne's asymptotically distribution-free (ADF) criteria for SEM. Several models or groups can be analyzed simultaneously. Faced with missing data, Amos provides estimation by ML (not by listwise or pairwise deletion, or using the mean). Amos can test the multivariate normality as well as the univariate normality of observed variables, and tries to identify the outliers. The graphic output provided by Amos can be directly imported into other programs such as word processors. Sometimes it is preferable to use Amos rather than traditional techniques like SPSS to do simple things, such as the estimation or test of means or variances, because Amos can better deal with missing data. This chapter is concerned with fundamental concepts related to modeling with Amos.

1.3.1 Variables and Their Classification

A variable is a property which can take on two or more values. In applied linguistics, variables include the type of corpus, genre of text, language style, sentence length, word length, text length, users' language proficiency/gender/age/group, and so on. There are so many variables that no one can list all of them. Variables can be classified in different ways.

1.3.1.1 Categorical vs. continuous

A categorical variable has a limited number of possible levels, while a continuous variable has an infinite number of possible values. For example, the type of corpus may be a categorical variable when it is classified into the corpus of native language and the corpus of translated language (2 levels). Users' language proficiency can be a continuous variable when it is measured in terms of test scores.

Categorical variables can be further divided into ordinal and normal variables. Ordinal variables have values which assign orders or ranks to objects or individuals, according to the degree which they have the quality of interest to. The values of normal variables are simply labels to classify things. For example, gender is a normal variable. We use males or females simply to group people. There is no difference in ranks between males and females. Academic grade, if represented by ranks such as A+, A, B+ and B, is an ordinal variable. The values can be put in a sequence like A+ > A > B+ > B.

Different researchers may treat the same variable in different ways, and therefore, a variable could be continuous in one study but ordinal in another.

1.3.1.2 Observed vs. unobserved

Observed variables are directly measured and listed in the data sets for analysis. Unobserved variables (latent variables, or factors) are hypothetic constructs that cannot be observed and therefore cannot be directly measured. Researchers have to define unobserved variables in terms of behaviors that can represent them. When we measure an observed behavior, we are directly measuring an observed variable but indirectly measuring an unobserved variable (Byrne, 2010). The observed variables corresponding to an unobserved variable are called indicators of the unobserved variable. For example, language test scores can be used as indicators of language competence.

1.3.1.3 Exogenous vs. endogenous

Exogenous variables are independent of any other variables in an SEM model. Their variances are only accounted for by factors outside the model. Endogenous variables are dependent on other variables. Their variances can be explained by variables in the model.

1.3.2 Sample Size

Needless to say, you can draw a confident conclusion about the characteristics of the population if you have studied every member of the population. But the time, money and effort involved may prevent a researcher from studying all the members in the population. One can only study a sample—a subset of the population, and then generalize the finding to the whole population. In SEM, the larger the sample size is, the more accurate the parameter estimation is. A more complex model or a model with more parameters to be estimated requires a larger sample size. The non-normal distribution of population requires a relatively large sample size. As a rule of thumb, the sample size should be no less than 10 times (ideally no less than 20 times) of the number of parameters to be estimated when ML is used for estimation. It has been found that a moderate sample size is about 200 in published studies using SEM. But estimation with methods other than ML generally requires a much larger sample size than 200 (Kline, 2011). For the illustration purpose, examples involving raw (simulated) data in later chapters of this book are all based on minimized sample sizes.

1.3.3 Distribution Requirement

If you use ML estimation or generalized least-squares estimation, the observed variables should be in the multivariate normal distribution. If some exogenous variables are measured exactly or fixed or known in advance (for example, experimental conditions, or predictors in regression analysis), they can have any distribution if 1) other variables are in the normal distribution with the same conditional variance-covariance matrix (regardless of the values of those exactly measured variables), and 2) other variables have a linear relationship with those variables.

Skewness and kurtosis can be used to judge the shape of the distribution. The absolute value of skewness greater than 3, or that of kurtosis greater than 8 (no universally agreed golden rule) indicates non-normal distribution. Distribution problem is sometimes caused by outliers, including univariate outliers and multivariate outliers. Univariate outliers are cases with values more than 3 standard deviations from the mean, and multivariate outliers are cases with an unusually great Mahalanobis distance ($p_2<0.05$; available in Amos output). If the required normality is not satisfied, we can 1) remove the outliers; 2) specify the outliers to equal the next extreme value within 3 standard deviations from the mean; or 3) transform the values of the non-normal variables (add a constant to all the values to make the smallest value positive, and replace all the values with their square roots or log values). For variables with extremely high scores, base = 10 is preferable for obtaining the log values; otherwise base = 2.718,28 will suffice.

1.3.4 Acceptable File Formats

The data must be processed in an appropriate format before they can be imported to Amos for analysis. Amos is compatible with many data formats. The following are some frequently used ones.

A. SPSS files with raw data (Figure 1.31)

	VAR_1	VAR_2	VAR_3	VAR_4	VAR_5
1	1	1	2	4	2
2	4	2	3	3	1
3	2	4	5	2	3
4	3	1	2	1	4
5	3	2	1	1	1

Figure 1.31 File format supported by Amos: Raw data in SPSS

B. SPSS files with correlations and standard deviations (means optional) (Figure 1.32)

	rowtype_	varname_	VAR_1	VAR_2	VAR_3	VAR_4	VAR_5
1	n		200	200	200	200	200
2	corr	VAR_1	1.00				
3	corr	VAR_2	0.31	1.00			
4	corr	VAR_3	0.33	0.27	1.00		
5	corr	VAR_4	0.42	0.35	0.19	1.00	
6	corr	VAR_5	0.15	0.23	0.24	0.36	1.00
7	stddev		0.66	0.58	0.55	0.59	0.71
8	mean		2.75	3.00	2.77	3.10	4.00

Figure 1.32 File format supported by Amos: Correlations with standard deviations in SPSS

C. Text files with raw data (tab-delimited) (Figure 1.33)

文件(F) 编辑(E) 格式(O) 查看(V) 帮助(H)

```
VAR_1	VAR_2	VAR_3	VAR_4	VAR_5
1	1	2	4	2
4	2	3	3	1
2	4	5	2	3
3	1	2	1	4
3	2	1	1	1
```

Figure 1.33 File format supported by Amos: Raw data in text

D. Text files of correlation matrix with standard deviations (comma-delimited; means optional) (Figure 1.34)

```
文件(F) 编辑(E) 格式(O) 查看(V) 帮助(H)
rowtype_,varname_,VAR_1,VAR_2,VAR_3,VAR_4,VAR_5
n,xx,200,200,200,200,200
corr,VAR_1,1.00
corr,VAR_2,0.31,1.00
corr,VAR_3,0.33,0.27,1.00
corr,VAR_4,0.42,0.35,0.19,1.00
corr,VAR_5,0.15,0.23,0.24,0.36,1.00
stddev,,0.66,0.58,0.55,0.59,0.71
mean,,2.75,3.00,2.77,3.10,4.00
```

Figure 1.34 File format supported by Amos: Correlations with standard deviations in text

E. Excel files with raw data (Figure 1.35)

	A	B	C	D	E
1	VAR_1	VAR_2	VAR_3	VAR_4	VAR_5
2	1	1	2	4	2
3	4	2	3	3	1
4	2	4	5	2	3
5	3	1	2	1	4
6	3	2	1	1	1

Figure 1.35 File format supported by Amos: Raw data in Excel

F. Excel files with correlations and standard deviations (means optional) (Figure 1.36)

	B	C	D	E	F	G
1	varname_	VAR_1	VAR_2	VAR_3	VAR_4	VAR_5
2		200	200	200	200	200
3	VAR_1	1.00				
4	VAR_2	0.31	1.00			
5	VAR_3	0.33	0.27	1.00		
6	VAR_4	0.42	0.35	0.19	1.00	
7	VAR_5	0.15	0.23	0.24	0.36	1.00
8		0.66	0.58	0.55	0.59	0.71
9		2.75	3.00	2.77	3.10	4.00

Figure 1.36 File format supported by Amos: Correlations with standard deviations in Excel

1.3.5 Graphic Tools and Path Diagrams

1.3.5.1 Graphic tools

When you run the Amos Graphics, the following window will appear (Figure 1.37).

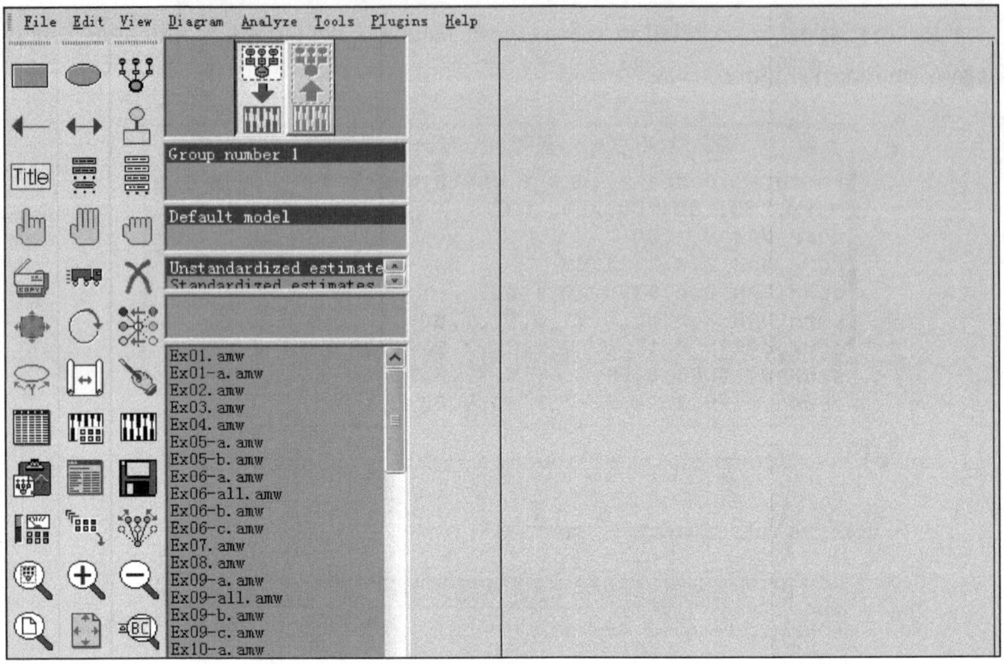

Figure 1.37 Amos Graphics window

On the left side of the window are the icons of frequently used tools. The functions of the tools are described in the following (Table 1.5).

Table 1.5 Frequently used tools in Amos Graphics

Tools	Functions
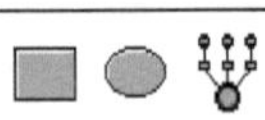	Draw observed variables (1st); draw unobserved variables (2nd); draw an unobserved variable and add indicators (3rd)
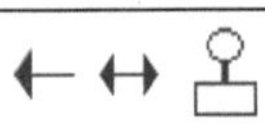	Draw single-headed arrows for regressions (1st); draw double-headed arrows for covariances (2nd); add indicators to a variable (3rd)
	Click in the drawing area to add a title to a path diagram
	List the variables in the model; you can drag the names to the diagram to replace existing variable names
	List the variables in the data set; you can drag the names to the diagram to replace existing variable names, or drag the names to the blank area to display observed variables
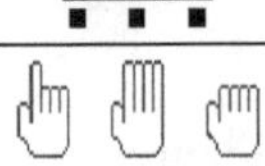	Select one or all, or deselect the object(s) in the drawing area, as indicated by the three icons respectively

Continued

Tools	Functions
	Drag an object to duplicate it
	Drag an object to move it
	Click an object to delete it
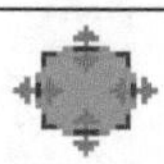	Drag an object to change its shape
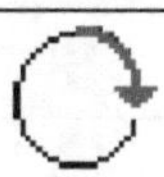	Click a latent variable to rotate its indicators
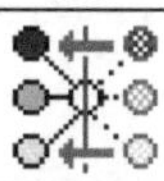	Click a latent variable to reflect its indicators
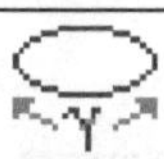	Move parameters
	Drag any section of the drawing area to reposition the path diagram as a whole
	Click an object to reposition the connecting arrows in a way intended to be aesthetically pleasing
	Select data files to be analyzed with the model
	"Display Analysis Properties" dialogue box
	Calculate estimates or run the analysis
	Copy the diagram for use in pasting
	View text output after running an analysis
	Save the diagram and the setting
	"Open the Object Properties" dialogue box
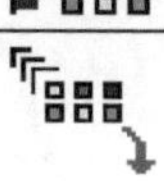	Select properties and duplicate them by drag from one object to another

Continued

Tools	Functions
	Preserve the original symmetries when moving or changing the shape of an object
	Zoom in on a selected portion
	Enlarge or minimize the diagram
	Display the whole diagram on one page
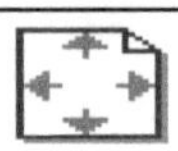	Change the size of the diagram
	Enlarge a portion of the path diagram for careful examination
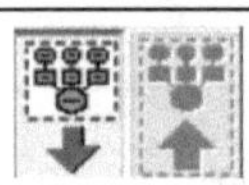	View the path diagram input or adjust the specification (1st); view the path diagram output (2nd)

For every icon, you have to click it first and then use it in the drawing area.

1.3.5.2 Path diagrams

In the Amos Graphics window, a path diagram is used to specify a model. In the drawing area, WHAT YOU SEE IS WHAT YOU GET. If you connect two exogenous variables with a double-headed arrow, you are requiring Amos to calculate the covariance or correlation between them; if two exogenous variables are not connected, you assume that the correlation is zero. Single-headed arrows are used to indicate regression. Figure 1.38 is an example of path diagram, in which the VAR_A is regressed on VAR_B and VAR_C. The "*e*" signifies all sources of variation of VAR_A which can not be accounted by VAR_B and VAR_C.

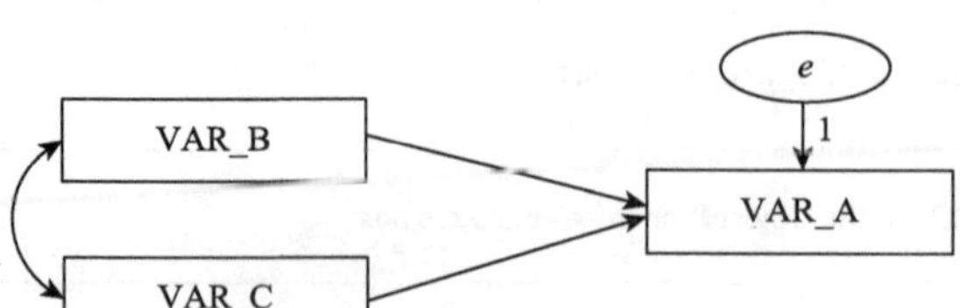

Figure 1.38　Illustration of a path diagram

To draw the path diagram, you have to run the Amos Graphics. Click [rectangle icon] and draw three rectangles in the drawing area; click [ellipse icon] and draw an ellipse; click ← or ↔ to connect the variables (Figure 1.39).

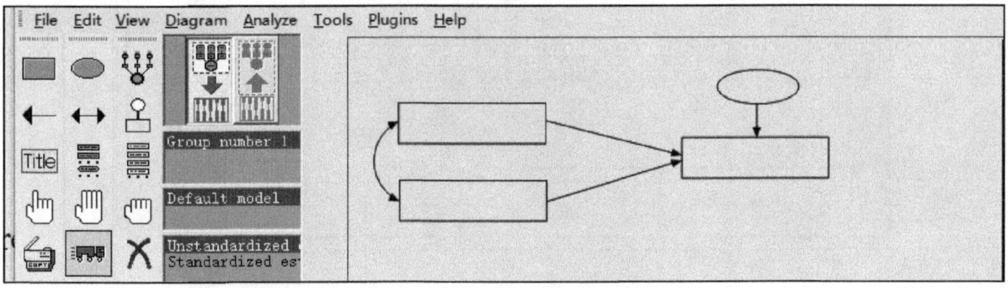

Figure 1.39 Drawing the figures connected by arrows

Right-click a figure and select “Object Properties” from the pop-up menu. Click the “Text” tab, and type the name for a variable. While keeping the dialogue box open, you can click other rectangles or the ellipse and enter the name in the “Variable name” text box (Figure 1.40).

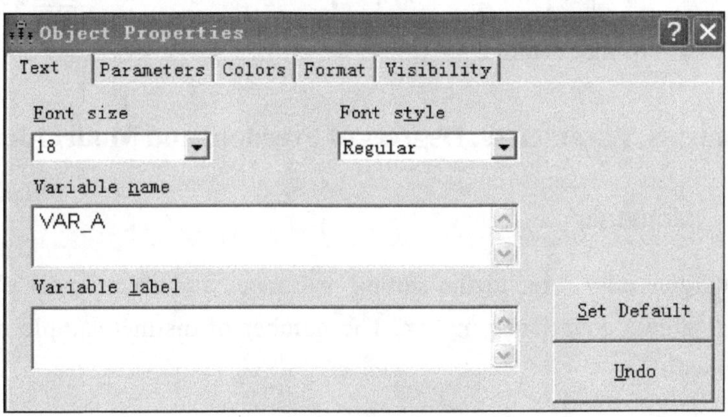

Figure 1.40 Naming the variables

While keeping the dialogue box open, click the “Parameters” tab. Click the arrow from *e* to VAR_A, and type “1” in the “Regression weight” text box (Figure 1.41). Close the dialogue box, and you will get the complete path diagram.

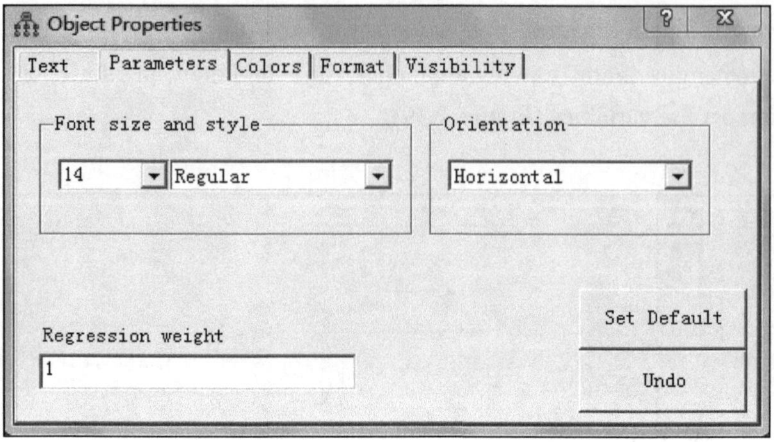

Figure 1.41 Specifying the regressing weight

If necessary, you can further adjust the path diagram (for example, you can use the  to move an object, use the  to adjust the size and shape of an object, or use the  to drag the properties of one object to another).

There are of course alternative methods to produce the path diagram. For example, when one rectangle or ellipse is drawn, you can use the  to duplicate the figure by dragging it, or use the  to add a unique variable. If you click , you can drag the variable names to the rectangles.

1.3.6 Moments, Parameters, Degrees of Freedom and Model Identification

1.3.6.1 Moments

Moments generally refer to the sample variances and covariances. They are the entries in the sample covariance matrix. The number of distinct sample moments can be calculated with

$$m = v(v+1)/2$$

where v is the number of observed variables. For example, when 10 observed variables are involved in a model, the number of distinct sample moments is $10(10+1)/2 = 55$. If means are estimated, the moments also include the means. When several groups are analyzed simultaneously, the number of distinct sample moments refers to the total number across all groups.

1.3.6.2 Parameters

Parameters refer to the statistical characteristics of a population. The number of distinct parameters to be estimated in a model is the total number of variances of exogenous variables, covariances and regression weights (also called path coefficients, factor loadings). Means of exogenous variables and intercepts of endogenous variables are included if they are estimated in the model. Parameters set at a fixed value are not counted. Several parameters specified to be equal are counted as 1 parameter. When several groups are analyzed simultaneously, the number of distinct parameters to be estimated refers to the total number across all groups.

1.3.6.3 Degrees of freedom

Degrees of freedom (*df*) are the difference between the number of distinct sample moments and the number of distinct parameters to be estimated.

1.3.6.4 Model identification

A model is not identified if it has one or more parameters which cannot be uniquely estimated. The following requirements are necessary for a model to be identified.

Firstly, each unobserved variable should be assigned a measurement unit. This can be done by fixing the variance or one of the regression weights at an arbitrary positive value (usually a regression weight is fixed at 1; for an explorative factor analysis relying on specification search, the common factor variance is fixed at 1).

Secondly, the *df* should be equal to or greater than zero. Identified models are just identified with $df = 0$, and are overidentified with $df > 0$. Even all those requirements are satisfied, a model may still be unidentified for some unknown reasons. If a model is unidentified, Amos may display a warning message or some suggestions for achieving identification.

1.3.7 Model Fit Measures

Model fit measures are statistical indexes suggesting the degree to which a model is supported by the data. The following are some frequently used model fit measures (Arbuckle, 2006: 528-548). In the formulas, χ^2 is the chi-square of the default model (if there are different models, χ^2 is used for the tested model while χ_b^2 for the baseline model); q is the number of parameters to be estimated; $\hat{F}$ is the minimum value of the discrepancy function F; $\hat{F}_b$ is the minimum value of the discrepancy function of the baseline model; d is the *df* of the tested model; d_b is the *df* of the baseline model; NCP is the noncentrality parameter of the tested model; NCP_b is the noncentrality parameter of the baseline model; G is the number of groups; N is the sample size; $N^{(g)}$ is the number of observations in group g; $N^{(1)}$ is the number of observations when only one group is involved; $b^{(g)} = N^{(g)} - 1$; $p^{(g)}$ is the number of observed variables in group g.

A. Minimum discrepancy function (χ^2)

$$\chi^2 = (N-1)\hat{F}$$

A model is acceptable when the p value associated with χ^2 is greater than 0.05. When the sample size is very large, the χ^2 test may become significant even though the discrepancy is trivial. In such cases, we may retain the model based on the other acceptable indexes which are less sensitive to sample sizes. If the sample size is not very large, we should not ignore the χ^2 test and rely solely on other indexes.

B. Root mean square error of approximation (RMSEA)

RMSEA is a parsimony-adjusted index. It imposes a penalty for model complexity. RMSEA$\leqslant$0.05 (or 0.08, or 0.10) has been recommended as showing preferable model fit. An upper limit and a lower limit of the 90% confidence are usually reported with RMSEA.

$$\text{RMSEA} = \sqrt{\frac{\chi^2 - d}{d(N-1)}}$$

C. Goodness of fit index (GFI)

It is the proportion of covariances and variances of the sample that is accounted for by the model. GFI is an absolute fit index, ranging between 0 and 1. GFI approaching 1 indicates a better fit. This index is prone to the influence of sample size (tending to increase with the sample size).

$$\text{GFI} = 1 - \frac{\hat{F}}{\hat{F}_b}$$

D. Normed fit index (NFI)

NFI is the ratio of the difference between χ^2 and χ_b^2, to χ_b^2. This is an incremental fit index. An NFI no less than 0.90 indicates a close fit. In recent years, the cut-off point is stated to be NFI$\geqslant$0.95.

$$\text{NFI} = 1 - \frac{\chi^2}{\chi_b^2}$$

E. Non-normed fit index (NNFI)

NNFI, also called Tucker-Lewis index (TLI), is an improved version of NFI, with the *df* taken into consideration. The purpose is to overcome the influence of model complexity. NNFI with a value close to 0.95 suggests a close fit. But NNFI has the tendency to underestimate the model fit when the sample size is below 100.

$$\text{NNFI} = (\chi_b^2/d_b - \chi^2/d)/(\chi_b^2/d_b - 1)$$

F. Comparative fit index (CFI)

This is a revised form of the NFI which is less affected by sample size. It is the ratio of the difference in noncentrality between the baseline (independent) model and the tested model, to the noncentrality of the baseline model. CFI close to 0.95 suggests a good fit.

$$\text{CFI} = 1 - \frac{\max(\chi^2 - d, 0)}{\max(\chi_b^2 - d_b, 0)} = 1 - \frac{\text{NCP}}{\text{NCP}_b}$$

G. Akaike information criterion (AIC)

It is also called information criteria indexes. AIC is employed to compare models. The model with the smallest value is the best fitting and most parsimonious model.

$$\text{AIC} = \chi^2 + 2q$$

H. Consistent version of AIC (CAIC)

It is an improved version of AIC, which attempts to adjust for the size of the sample. This statistic gives a stronger penalty to the complexity of a model than AIC. The model with a smaller value is a better fitting one.

$$\text{CAIC} = \chi^2 + q(\ln N^{(1)} + 1)$$

I. Browne-Cudeck criterion (BCC)

BCC is also used for the evaluation of competing models, which has a stronger penalty for complex models than AIC. The model with a smaller value is a better fitting one.

$$\text{BCC} = \chi^2 + 2q\frac{\sum_{g=1}^{G} b^{(g)} \dfrac{p^{(g)}(p^{(g)}+3)}{N^{(g)} - p^{(g)} - 2}}{\sum_{g=1}^{G} p^{(g)}(p^{(g)}+3)}$$

J. Bayes information criterion (BIC)

In comparison with the AIC, BCC and CAIC, the BIC has a greater penalty to model complexity and, therefore, is in favor of a simple model. The model with a smaller value is a better fitting one.

$$\mathrm{BIC} = \chi^2 + q\ln(N^{(1)})$$

In addition to the indexes above, root mean square residual (RMR, with a smaller value indicating a better fit), incremental fit index (IFI, with a value closer to 1 indicating a better fit) and relative fit index (RFI, with a value closer to 1 indicating a better fit) are also used sometimes, which are not to be discussed in details here. Each fit index reflects one aspect of fit. We should take into consideration all of the indexes when evaluating model fit. The cutoff points mentioned above should not be taken as golden rules. There is still a lot of disagreements among experts. For the illustration purpose, in most of the examples of this book, only χ^2 is used as an indicator of model fit.

1.4 Summary

Applied linguistics is concerned with the application of linguistic theory to a particular field of study, specifically second language learning. SEM is a commonly used statistical method in applied linguistics. Big data corpora are important resources for research in applied linguistics, but they cannot be modeled with SEM directly. We can, however, extract valuable small data from the former. To extract small data from online data corpora, we have to grasp the searching skills related to each corpus; to extract small data from offline data corpora, we need to make use of various software tools. With the small data available, we can conduct SEM and reveal valuable relationships among the data, as will be shown in later chapters. Except for the cases in which the sources of the data are mentioned, all the data employed in examples are collected by the author in his research.

Chapter 2 Parameter Estimation and Test

In applied linguistics, we are frequently faced with the task of making inferences about the parameters. We may want to know whether the population mean, variance and covariance of one variable differ from those of another variable. These tasks can be completed with conventional programs such as SPSS, and they can also be completed with Amos. You may prefer to use Amos because it is not only convenient, but also capable of producing visual outputs.

2.1 Estimation of Parameters

Amos can be used to estimate the population covariances, correlations, means and variances. What you have to do is to import the data, draw a path diagram in which the variables are correlated, set the analysis properties, and run the analysis. Now the application will be illustrated by the following examples.

2.1.1 Estimation of Covariances and Correlations

2.1.1.1 Dataset and task

From a big data corpus, we can discover the frequencies of different words or strings. Table 2.1 compares some of the results of searching for "more * than" in different genres of the BNC and in the corpus of Ten-thousand English Compositions of Chinese Learners (TECCL). From the BNC, the frequencies involve those of spoken English (FR_SP), fiction English (FR_FI), magazine English (FR_MA) and newspaper English (FR_NE). For the TECCL corpus, there is no genre discrimination (frequency distribution in TECCL, namely FR_TE).

Table 2.1 The frequencies of "more * than" in different sections of English

Words/Symbols	FR_SP	FR_FI	FR_MA	FR_NE	FR_TE
More important than	42	63	50	51	117
More often than	20	46	49	26	7

Continued

Words/Symbols	FR_SP	FR_FI	FR_MA	FR_NE	FR_TE
More so than	23	27	24	28	0
More expensive than	22	8	20	14	16
More likely than	3	5	8	12	0
More complex than	8	8	6	3	1
More difficult than	11	22	13	14	8
More effective than	4	5	11	10	3
More powerful than	4	23	17	7	1
More quickly than	7	16	10	11	1

Source: https://www.english-corpora.org/bnc/; the TECCL was downloaded from http://corpus.bfsu.edu.cn/content/teccl-corpus [2019-05-08]

Now we want to examine whether the relative frequencies of those strings are similar in different sections of English. In other words, we are curious about whether a string occurring more frequently in one section also tends to occur more frequently in another section of English.

2.1.1.2 Modeling with Amos Graphics

In traditional statistics, a preferable way to find out the answer is to examine the correlation. In Amos, we can do it by estimating the covariances as well as the correlations. The following are the key steps involved.

A. Processing the data in a format acceptable to Amos

The data can be processed with the SPSS, Excel or Microsoft Notepad.

B. Importing the data files to Amos

Click “File” and then click “Data Files” (or click [icon]) (Figure 2.1).

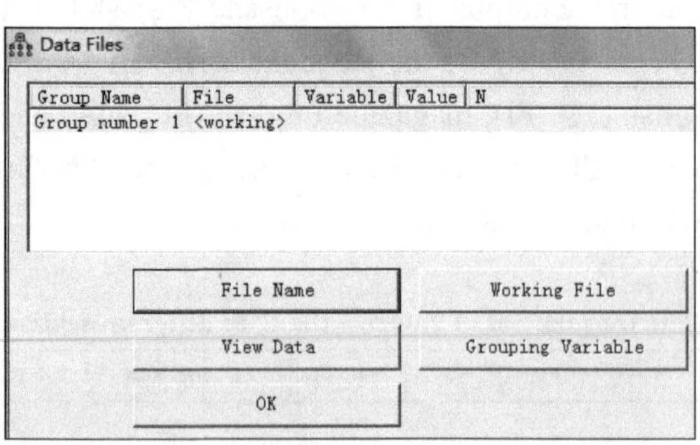

Figure 2.1 Importing the data files to Amos

Click “File Name” to select the file. If you want to see the data file, click “View Data”; if you are not interested in viewing the data, simply click “OK” to close the “Data Files” dialogue box.

C. Creating a path diagram

By using the Amos Graphics, we can easily create a path diagram (Figure 2.2).

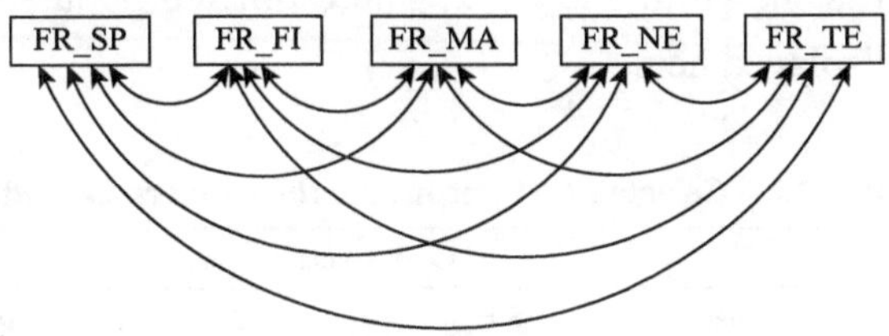

Figure 2.2 A path diagram for estimating covariances and correlations

D. Setting the analysis properties

We have to activate the “Analysis Properties” dialogue box, and click the “Estimation” tab. Then select “Maximum likelihood” (Figure 2.3). This is the preferable selection for general SEM.

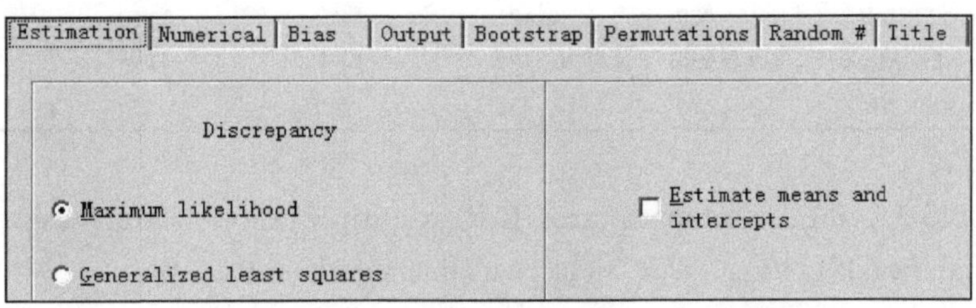

Figure 2.3 Setting the analysis properties for estimation

Next, click the “Output” tab, and select “Standardized estimates” “Covariances of estimates” “Correlations of estimates” (Figure 2.4).

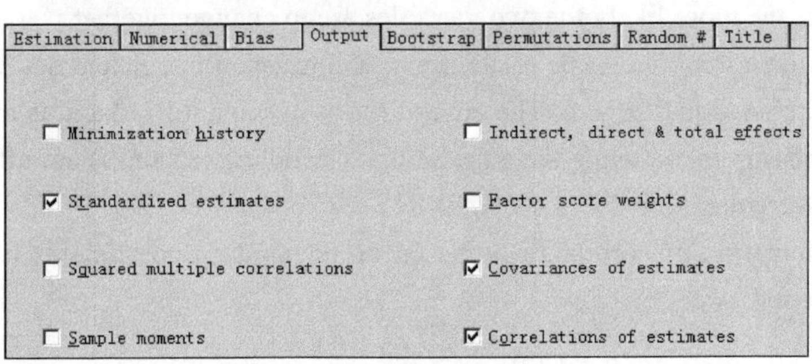

Figure 2.4 Setting the analysis properties for output

To run the analysis, click the icon in the Amos Graphics window (or click "Analyze" → "Calculate Estimates" in the Amos tool menu), and the estimation will be completed instantly.

2.1.1.3 Estimation results

The text output is shown in Table 2.2. The estimated population covariances and correlations are all displayed here.

Table 2.2 Selected text output for the concerned model

Variables	Covariances				Correlations
	Estimates	S.E.	C.R.	*p*	Estimates
FR_SP<-->FR_TE	330.740	173.410	1.907	0.056	0.824
FR_SP<-->FR_FI	169.680	90.747	1.870	0.062	0.797
FR_SP<-->FR_MA	147.380	77.339	1.906	0.057	0.822
FR_SP<-->FR_NE	143.860	70.875	2.030	0.042	0.919
FR_FI<-->FR_MA	255.360	125.525	2.034	0.042	0.923
FR_FI<-->FR_NE	213.120	107.443	1.984	0.047	0.881
FR_TE<-->FR_FI	462.480	257.885	1.793	0.073	0.746
FR_MA<-->FR_NE	175.020	89.481	1.956	0.050	0.860
FR_TE<-->FR_MA	347.980	209.129	1.664	0.096	0.667
FR_TE<-->FR_NE	382.560	198.437	1.928	0.054	0.839

In Table 2.2, S.E. is standard error, C.R. is critical ratio (= Estimates/S.E.), and p is the probability of getting a C.R. as large as that shown in the table.

Covariances and correlations both describe how one variable changes with another. A positive covariance or correlation coefficient suggests that the two variables have the tendency to change in the same direction. A negative coefficient suggests that the two variables tend to change in the opposite directions. The larger the absolute value of a coefficient is, the more likely the two variables are to change together.

Though describing the same relationship, a correlation coefficient and a covariance coefficient are not equal in size. The covariance is unstandardized and is influenced by the unit of measurement, while the correlation is standardized and is not affected by the scale of measurement.

The calculation of correlation is based on covariation coefficients (COV) which can be expressed as

$$\text{COV} = \frac{\sum(x-\bar{x})(y-\bar{y})}{n}$$

where x and y are the paired scores of the two variables, $\overline{x}$ and $\overline{y}$ are the means of the two distributions of scores, and n is the number of paired scores. Correlation coefficient can be expressed as

$$r=\frac{\sum\left(\frac{x-\overline{x}}{\sigma_x}\right)\left(\frac{y-\overline{y}}{\sigma_y}\right)}{n}=\frac{\sum(x-\overline{x})(y-\overline{y})}{n\sigma_x\sigma_y}$$

where σ_x is the sample standard deviation of the variable x, and σ_y is the sample standard deviation of the variable y.

The estimate of a parameter is significantly different from zero when p is equal to or smaller than 0.05. In the present example, half of the estimates of the covariances and correlations are significant. The estimates of the parameters can be displayed on the path diagram output. The unstandardized path diagram output displays the covariances, while the standardized path diagram shows the correlations between the variables. Figure 2.5 is a standardized output.

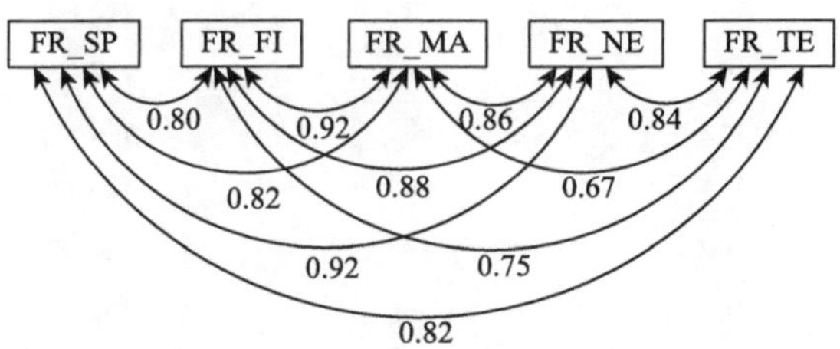

Figure 2.5 A standardized graphic output

Near the midpoint of a double-headed arrow is the correlation coefficients. From the correlations, we can infer that the Chinese students' compositions in the TECCL corpus and the different genres of English by native users tend to employ "more * than" in more or less similar relative frequencies. Native speakers' uses have higher correlations (0.80-0.92), while Chinese students' uses are not so highly correlated with the uses of native speakers (0.67-0.84).

2.1.2 Estimation of Variances and Means

2.1.2.1 Dataset and task

In a study, a group of university students were all required to produce two writings: an essay and a narration. Two corpora were created based on the essays and narrations.

The numbers of tokens and types in each writing were calculated. Table 2.3 shows the data of 30 students' writings, which are to be used to illustrate the estimation of means and variances.

Table 2.3 The frequency of tokens and types in the two writings

Number	TO_E (tokens in essay)	TY_E (types in essay)	TO_N (tokens in narration)	TY_N (types in narration)
1	120	64	104	56
2	216	136	200	104
3	184	104	168	96
4	184	120	176	96
5	176	104	160	96
6	184	104	176	104
7	184	112	168	96
8	160	96	144	80
9	144	72	128	64
10	136	72	112	48
11	144	64	152	80
12	152	88	144	72
13	152	80	136	72
14	160	88	144	80
15	160	104	152	80
16	168	104	144	88
17	184	88	176	96
18	168	96	152	88
19	168	104	160	96
20	176	112	152	88
21	176	96	160	96
22	176	112	160	88
23	176	104	168	104
24	176	104	160	96
25	184	112	160	104
26	184	112	176	88
27	184	112	168	96
28	192	112	176	96
29	192	120	168	88
30	200	128	192	104

2.1.2.2 Modeling with Amos Graphics

Now we will estimate the population means and variances. We have to process the data and import them to Amos, and then complete the following procedures.

A. Creating a path diagram

By using the Amos Graphics, we can create a path diagram very easily (Figure 2.6).

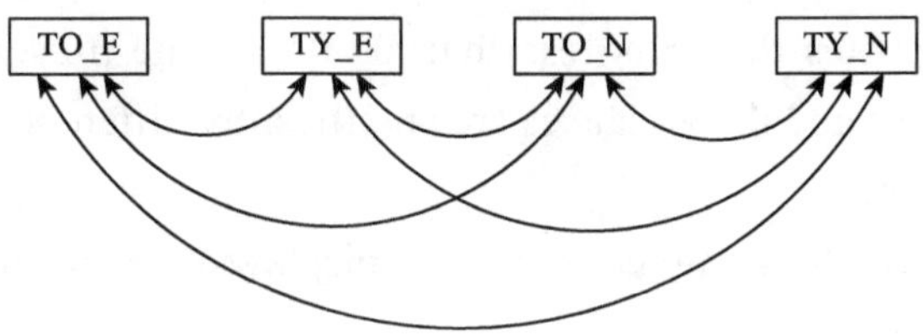

Figure 2.6 A path diagram for estimating means and variances

B. Setting the analysis properties

We have to activate the "Analysis Properties" dialogue box, and click the "Estimation" tab. Then select "Estimate means and intercepts". Next, click the "Output" tab and select "Standardized estimates" (Figure 2.7).

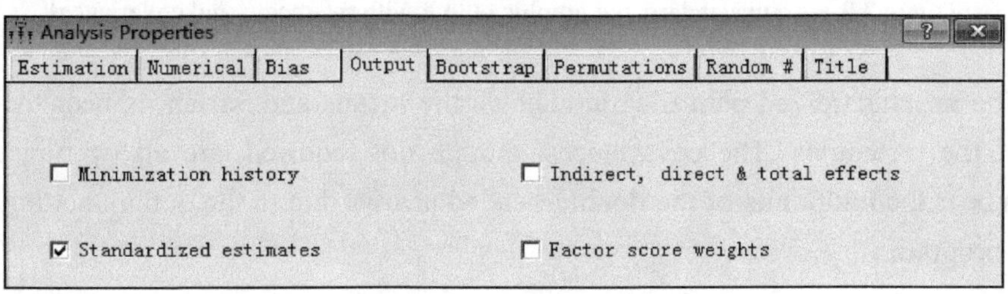

Figure 2.7 Setting the analysis properties for output

After the setting is finished, we can run the analysis, and the estimation will be completed in no time.

2.1.2.3 Estimation results

A. Text output

The text output is shown in Table 2.4. The estimated population means and variances are all displayed here.

Table 2.4 Selected output for a model estimating means and variances

Variables	Means				Variances			
	Estimates	S.E.	C.R.	*p*	Estimates	S.E.	C.R.	*p*
TO_E	172.000	3.654	47.072	***	387.200	101.684	3.808	***
TY_E	100.800	3.223	31.276	***	301.227	79.106	3.808	***
TO_N	157.867	3.776	41.803	***	413.582	108.612	3.808	***
TY_N	88.000	2.602	33.827	***	196.267	51.542	3.808	***

The "***" signifies that p is less than 0.001. In the present example, all the estimates of the means and the variances are significantly different from zero.

B. Graphic output

The estimates of the parameters can be displayed on the path diagram output (Figure 2.8).

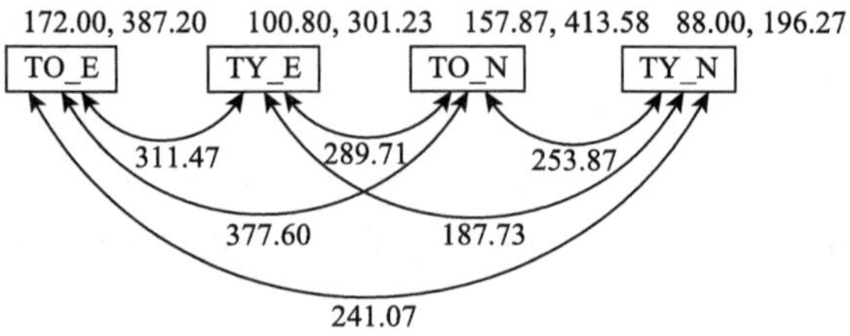

Figure 2.8 An unstandardized graphic output with the means and covariances

The unstandardized path diagram shows the means and variances near the upper side of the rectangles. The covariances, though not required, are also produced and shown near the midpoints of the double-headed arrows due to the default setting of the Amos program.

2.2 Test of Parameters

Amos provides convenient ways to test hypotheses about parameter differences. We have to assign the same label for parameters which are assumed to be equal. If the results show that the model is acceptable, we can infer that the parameters with the same label are not significantly different. Unacceptable results indicate that some parameters with the same label are significantly different. We can modify the model in Section 2.1.2 and repeat the analysis to find out which parameters are significantly different. Based on the dataset in Table 2.3, now we will further examine 1) whether the mean for TO_E is significantly different from that for TO_N, and 2) whether the mean for TY_E is significantly different from that for TY_N. In other words, we have to test two hypotheses: 1) Mean of TO_E = Mean of TO_N; 2) Mean of TY_E = Mean of TY_N.

2.2.1 Modeling and the Estimation Results

2.2.1.1 Modeling with Amos Graphics

To test the parameters, we have to begin with the modeling. The steps include 1) importing the well processed data file; 2) building a path diagram in the drawing area of the Amos Graphics window; 3) adding labels to the model; and 4) setting the analysis properties (in the "Analysis Properties" dialogue box, select "Estimate means and intercepts").

To add labels, we have to right-click the variable "TO_E", and select "Object Properties" in the pop-up menu. Then click the "Parameters" tab, and type "m_TO" (an arbitrary label for the mean of token) in the "Mean" text box. While keeping the "Object Properties" dialogue box open, click "TO_N" and type "m_TO" as the mean. Now TO_E and TO_N share the same mean label. In similar ways, specify TY_E and TY_N to share the same mean label "m_TY". The model with labels should be like the following (Figure 2.9).

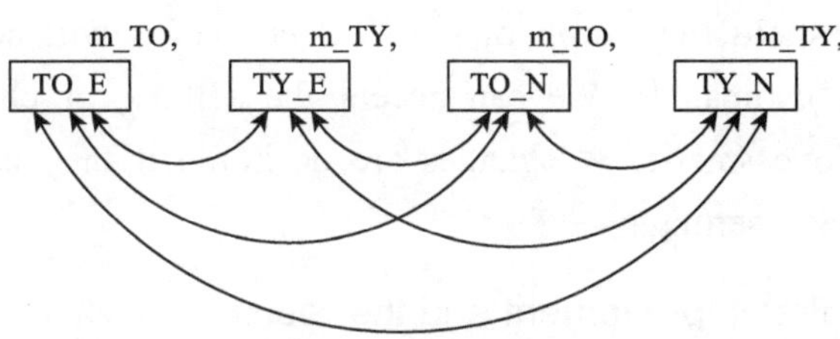

Figure 2.9 A path diagram with labels for testing parameter differences

The label names are arbitrary. So you can use other characters as well. The essential requirement is that parameters assumed to be equal must have the same label.

2.2.1.2 Estimation results

Run the analysis, and we can see the text output. Displayed below is a summary of the estimation results (Table 2.5).

Table 2.5 Summary for a model testing parameter differences

Variables	Values
Number of distinct sample moments	14
Number of distinct parameters to be estimated	12
df	2
χ^2	49.053
p	0.000

If means are not estimated, the number of distinct sample moments is

$$m = v(v + 1)/2 = 4(4 + 1)/2 = 10$$

where v is the number of observed variables, but here we estimated the means. Together with the four means, the total number of moments is $10 + 4 = 14$. Since we suppose that in the population 1) the mean of TO_E and that of TO_N are equal, and 2) the mean of TY_E and that of TY_N are equal, the parameters are less than the moments ($14 - 2 = 12$).

With $\chi^2 = 49.053$ ($p = 0.000 < 0.05$), the model is not acceptable. In other words, it is not acceptable to simultaneously assume 1) TO_E and TO_N share the same mean, and 2) TY_E and TY_N share the same mean.

2.2.2 Model Improvements and the Results

To improve the model fitting, we can check the "Modification Indices" (M.I.) under "Output" in the "Analysis Properties". The default number "4" corresponding to the M.I. is the threshold (a χ^2 drop of 4 or larger than 4 will be reported when a parameter is freely estimated). We can accept the setting, or change it to smaller numbers if we believe smaller χ^2 changes are desirable if they can be achieved by changing the parameter settings.

2.2.2.1 The first improvement and the results

A. Producing the M.I. with the default threshold

As the first attempt to improve the model, we can simply accept the default M.I. threshold of 4, and run the analysis again. In the text output, we will see the M.I. related to the parameter of the population mean (Table 2.6).

Table 2.6 Modification information for a model testing parameter differences with the M.I. threshold of 4

Variable	M.I.	Par change
TO_N	6.704	–4.274

The M.I. provides information for the improvement of the model. Here only one M.I. is displayed. The information suggests that χ^2 may drop at least by 6.704 if the mean of TO_N is freely estimated. Simultaneously, the new mean may become smaller by approximately 4.274 than the current value.

B. Modifying the model based on the modification information

Since the m_TO (attached to both TO_E and TO_N) is used to connect TO_E and TO_N, directing the Amos program to estimate a mean value shared by the two variables, we have to remove the label m_TO for the mean of TO_N so that Amos can freely estimate the parameter (in cases when two or more M.I. are displayed, we should first alter the setting related to larger or the largest M.I.). When the estimation of the mean of TO_N is independent of the estimation of the mean of TO_E, the label m_TO for TO_E can also be removed since it no longer has any impact on TO_E. The modified model is like the following (Figure 2.10).

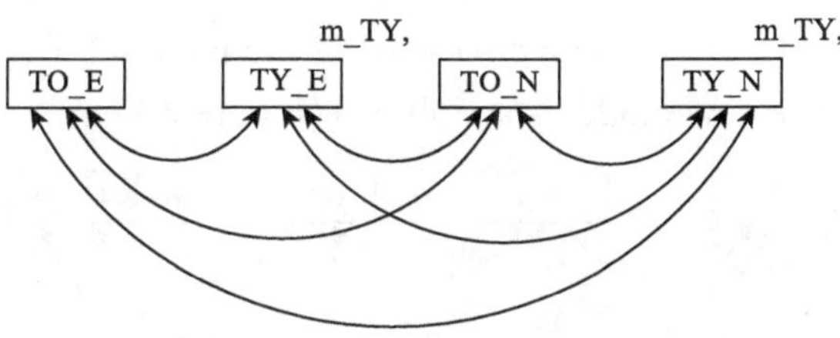

Figure 2.10 The first improvement of a model testing parameter differences

C. Estimation results for the modified model

To examine the fitness of the modified model, we have to repeat the analysis and examine the results (Table 2.7).

Table 2.7 Summary for a model testing parameter differences after the first improvement

Variables	Values
Number of distinct sample moments	14
Number of distinct parameters to be estimated	13
df	1
χ^2	26.687
p	0.000

The results show that the model is still unacceptable.

2.2.2.2 The second improvement and the results

A. Producing the M.I. with a smaller threshold

Since no M.I. is displayed in the text output, we should change the default M.I.

threshold of "4" to a smaller value so as to make the model more sensitive. Now we can simply try the number "2". Run the analysis again, and we can obtain the refreshed M.I. (Table 2.8).

Table 2.8 Modification information for a model testing parameter differences with the M.I. threshold of 2

Variables	M.I.	Par change
TY_E	3.443	2.652
TY_N	2.724	–2.098

These values suggest that χ^2 may drop by 3.443 if we freely estimate the mean for TY_E, and drop by 2.724 if we freely estimate the mean for TY_N.

B. Modifying the model based on the refreshed M.I.

Taking the refreshed M.I. into consideration, now we should first remove the mean label m_TY for TY_E. We can also remove the label for TY_N due to its loss of constraining power. The new model is as follows (Figure 2.11).

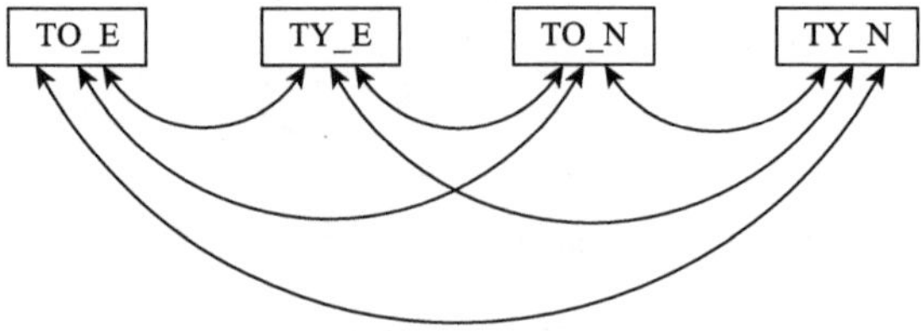

Figure 2.11 The second improvement of a model testing parameter differences

C. Estimation results for the secondly modified model

Now repeat the analysis for the model without any shared parameter labels and examine the results (Table 2.9).

Table 2.9 Summary for a model testing parameter differences after the second improvement

Variables	Values
Number of distinct sample moments	14
Number of distinct parameters to be estimated	14
df	0
χ^2	0.000

Since there is no restriction on the model and all the population parameters corresponding to the sample moments are estimated, *df* is zero. χ^2 = 0.000 suggests that the estimated model (default model) has no discrepancy from the data. In other words, the model fits the data perfectly. Of course, there could not be any discrepancy because we impose no constraints on the model. The model with $df = 0$ is called a saturated model, which always has χ^2 of zero.

Now we can arrive at the conclusion to the task at hand. The mean for TO_E is significantly different from that for TO_N, and the mean for TY_E is significantly different from that for TY_N.

2.3 Summary

Amos provides convenient and effective ways for parameter estimation and test. The first step is to draw a path diagram with the Amos Graphics. Then open the "Analysis Properties" panel and complete the setting. ML estimation is the preferable algorithm for producing the discrepancy. If an incomplete dataset is involved in the analysis, means and intercepts must be estimated. The results can include text outputs, as well as graphic outputs. Standardized/unstandardized graphic outputs can visually display standardized/unstandardized parameter estimates. To test parameters, we may impose constraints on the parameters and examine the fit after the analysis. M.I. can be used to improve the model fit.

Chapter 3 Path Models

Path models are also called path analysis models, which focus on developing explanatory relationships between observed variables. The exogenous (independent) variables are assumed to have no measurement errors. The variance of the endogenous (dependent) variables is assumed to be partly explained by the predictors (explanatory observed variables) and partly explained by unknown factors, including measurement errors. In the model equation, all the unknown explanatory factors related to an endogenous variable are represented by an error variable. No substantial latent variable is included in a path analysis model.

To illustrate the nature of dependency of endogenous variables on predictors and error variables, we will use a simple example. Suppose we have four observed variables, namely x_1, x_2, y_1 and y_2. The variables x_1 and x_2 are used to predict y_1 and y_2, as can be shown in the following path diagram (Figure 3.1).

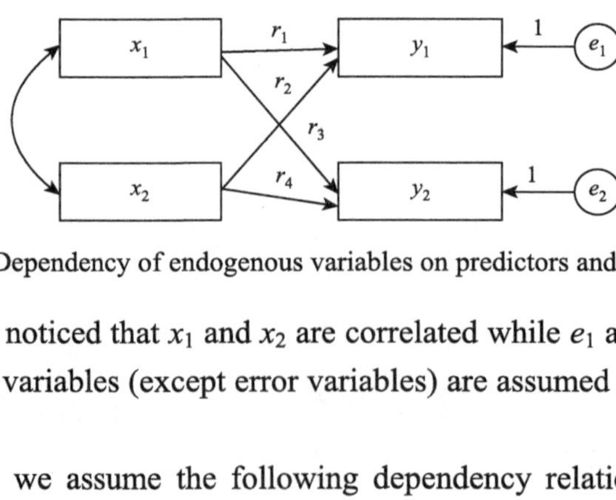

Figure 3.1 Dependency of endogenous variables on predictors and error variables

You may have noticed that x_1 and x_2 are correlated while e_1 and e_2 are not. This is because exogenous variables (except error variables) are assumed to be inter-correlated by default in SEM.

In this model, we assume the following dependency relationships (r_1 to r_4 are regression weights).

$$y_1 = x_1 \cdot r_1 + x_2 \cdot r_2 + e_1$$
$$y_2 = x_1 \cdot r_3 + x_2 \cdot r_4 + e_2$$

3.1 Types of Elementary Path Models

There are various sub-types of path models, and they can be classified in different ways. In this book, path models are distinguished between recursive and nonrecursive ones.

3.1.1 Recursive Path Models

Recursive path models do not involve feedback loops. In other words, there are no variables having effects on each other. The following are some elementary recursive path models that can be used to constitute complex ones.

3.1.1.1 Recursive path models involving a single predictor

The diagram shown below illustrates a recursive path model with a single predictor (cause) named variable_1, which is used to predict variable_2. The model can also be interpreted as variable_1 causing variable_2, or variable_2 depending on variable_1. An unknown variable *e* (error term) is connected with variable_2 by a single-headed arrow, indicating that part of the variance of variable_2 is accounted for by *e*. The "1" near the arrow from *e* to variable_2 is a specified regression weight (path coefficient), which is used to make the model identified (Figure 3.2).

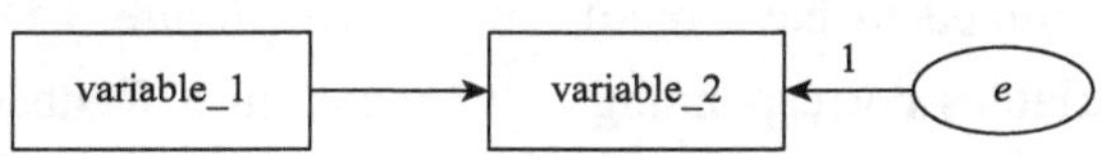

Figure 3.2 A path model with a single predictor

3.1.1.2 Recursive path models involving multiple predictors

The following path diagram is an example of recursive path models involving multiple predictors (causes). Here variable_1 and variable_2 are used to predict variable_3 (Figure 3.3).

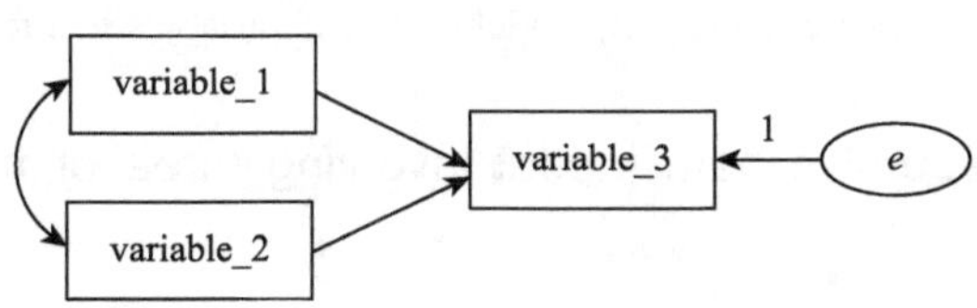

Figure 3.3 A path model with multiple predictors

3.1.1.3 Recursive path models involving indirect predictors

Here is an example of recursive path models involving indirect predictors (causes).

Variable_1 predicts variable_3 via variable_2 (Figure 3.4).

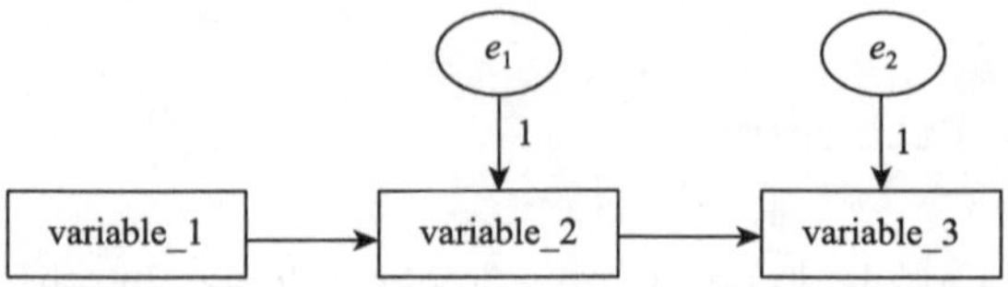

Figure 3.4 A path model with indirect predictors

3.1.2 Nonrecursive Path Models

Models involving feedback loops are called nonrecursive path models. In a nonrecursive path model, there are variables which have effects on each other or on one another. The effects are indicated by the feedback loops.

3.1.2.1 Nonrecursive path model involving two variables in a feedback loop

The following model is an example of the nonrecursive path model, in which a feedback loop exists between two variables, namely variable_3 and variable_4. The two variables are assumed to have mutual influence (Figure 3.5). In a nonrecursive model, the error variables corresponding to variables in a feedback loop are usually assumed to be correlated. This is because variables in a feedback loop are likely to share unknown causes.

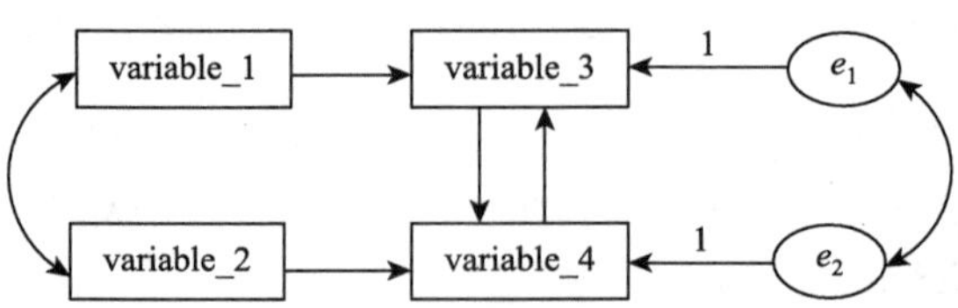

Figure 3.5 A nonrecursive path model with two variables in a feedback loop

3.1.2.2 Nonrecursive path model involving three or more variables in a feedback loop

A nonrecursive path model may also have a feedback loop in which more than two variables are involved. In the following example, variable_1, variable_3 and variable_4 are involved in the same feedback loop. The directions of the arrows in the loop indicate the paths of influence (Figure 3.6).

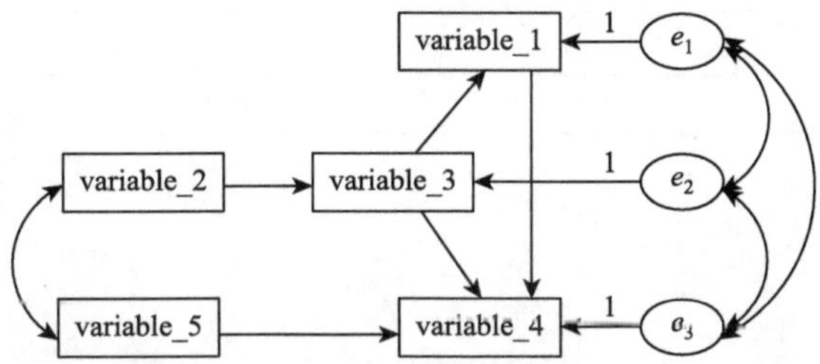

Figure 3.6 A nonrecursive path model with three variables in a feedback loop

3.2 Examples of the Analysis of Path Models

3.2.1 A Path Model for Linear Regression

With the regression analysis, we can decide whether and how a variable can be predicted by other relevant variables. The results are quite similar to those obtained from the conventional analysis. Now the application will be illustrated by the following examples.

3.2.1.1 Dataset and task

A group of students were involved in an oral interview, and the speaking self-efficacy (SSE) of each student was also investigated with a questionnaire. Their speeches were converted into texts, which were used to create a corpus. The tokens (TOK) and types (TYP) in the corpus were calculated. The regression of the SSE on the TOK and TYP is to be examined here. For the illustration purpose, the data of 30 students will be analyzed (Table 3.1).

Table 3.1 Data for a path model for linear regression

Number	TOK	TYP	SSE
1	115	58	55
2	127	67	56
3	123	63	57
4	123	65	58
5	122	63	59
6	123	63	60
7	123	64	61
8	120	62	62
9	118	59	63

Continued

Number	TOK	TYP	SSE
10	117	59	73
11	118	58	75
12	119	61	76
13	119	60	77
14	120	61	78
15	120	63	78
16	121	63	79
17	123	61	79
18	121	62	80
19	121	63	81
20	122	64	83
21	122	62	84
22	122	64	84
23	122	63	85
24	122	63	85
25	123	64	87
26	123	64	89
27	123	64	91
28	124	64	91
29	124	65	92
30	125	66	93

3.2.1.2 Modeling with Amos Graphics

We have to process the data in a format acceptable to Amos, import the data file to Amos, and create a path diagram like the following (Figure 3.7).

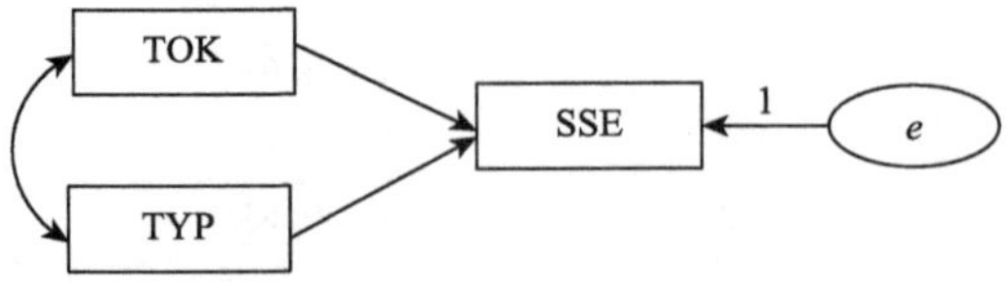

Figure 3.7 A path model used for linear regression

Then set the analysis properties. We have to open the "Analysis Properties" dialogue box and click the "Output" tab. Here "Minimization history" is selected by default. We have to further select "Standardized estimates" and "Squared multiple correlations" (Figure 3.8).

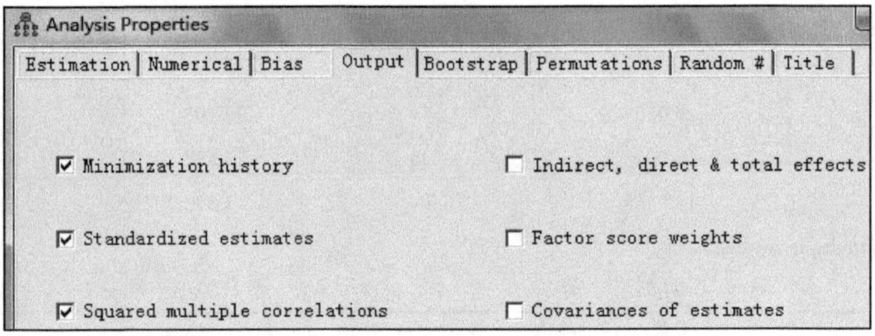

Figure 3.8 Specifying the output for a path model used for linear regression

When the above setting is done, close the "Analysis Properties" dialogue box and run the analysis.

3.2.1.3 Estimation results in text

Displayed in Table 3.2 and Table 3.3 is the selected text output, including the summary and parameter estimates for this simple path model analysis.

Table 3.2 Summary for a path model used for linear regression

Variables	Values
Number of distinct sample moments	14
Number of distinct parameters to be estimated	14
df	0
χ^2	0.000

Table 3.3 Selected estimation results for a path model used for linear regression

Variables	Estimates	S.E.	C.R.	*p*
Regression weights				
SSE<---TOK	0.621	2.156	0.288	0.773
SSE<---TYP	0.635	2.445	0.260	0.795
Standardized regression weights				
SSE<---TOK	0.127			
SSE<---TYP	0.114			
Covariances				
TOK<-->TYP	4.867	1.341	3.629	***

Continued

Variables	Estimates	S.E.	C.R.	*p*
Correlations				
TOK<-->TYP	0.912			
Variances				
TOK	6.050	1.589	3.808	***
TYP	4.707	1.236	3.808	***
e	137.268	36.048	3.808	***
Squared multiple correlations				
SSE	0.056			

Now we will examine the meaning of the output.

A. Model summary

The number of distinct sample moments is reported to be 6. You can calculate it with

$$m = v(v + 1)/2 = 3(3 + 1)/2 = 6$$

where v is the number of observed variables. The 6 moments include the variances of all the observed variables (3), and the covariances between those variables (3). The number of distinct parameters to be estimated is reported to be 6. You can also check it. It includes 3 variances (the variances of the 3 exogenous variables, namely TOK, TYP and e), 1 covariance coefficient, and 2 regression weights. The *df* is zero. This is a saturated (just-identified) model. Every parameter is freely estimated. No hypothesis is being tested. A saturated model always has a perfect fit ($\chi^2 = 0$).

B. Regression weights

In the present example, we are primarily concerned with the regression of SSE on TOK and TYP. The estimates of the regression weights suggest that the regression of SSE on TOK and TYP is not significant. A 1-point increase on TOK predicts a 0.621-point increase on SSE, and a 1-point increase on TYP predicts a 0.635-point increase on SSE.

The standardized regression weights are the regression weights divided by their standard deviations. The values are not influenced by the scale of measurement. In this example, the standardized regression weight of SSE on TOK is 0.127, which suggests that an increase of 1 standardized deviation on TOK predicts an increase of 0.127 standardized deviation on SSE. The standardized regression weight of SSE on TYP can be explained in similar ways.

C. Squared multiple correlation

Squared multiple correlation indicates the proportion of variance of an endogenous variable explained by all the predictors. It can be calculated as follows.

$$R_m^2 = 1 - \sigma_{\text{err}} / \sigma_{\text{en}}$$

where σ_{err} is the variance of the error variable, and σ_{en} is the variance of the relevant endogenous variable. The $\sigma_{\text{err}}/\sigma_{\text{en}}$ refers to the variance accounted for by the error terms.

In the present example, the estimated value of squared multiple correlation is 0.056, which means that about 5.6% of the variance of SSE can be accounted for by TOK and TYP. We can infer that 94.4% of the variance of SSE is explained by unknown factors (*e* in the model).

D. Variances of the exogenous variables

Additional outputs are the variances of the exogenous variables. Examining the variances, you can get a general idea of the degree of dispersion of raw scores of each variable. For example, TOK has a larger variance, which means that the data of TOK has a higher degree of dispersion than the data of TYP.

3.2.1.4 Estimation results in graphics

Click the  in the Amos Graphics window, and you can examine the path diagram outputs (Figure 3.9 and Figure 3.10). Click the "Unstandardized estimates" or "Standardized estimates" in a panel to the left of the drawing area of the Amos Graphics window, you can switch between the two types of outputs.

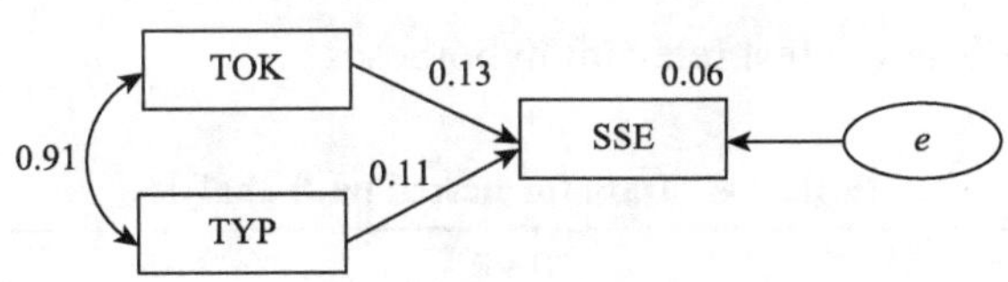

Figure 3.9 Standardized graphic output for a path model used for linear regression

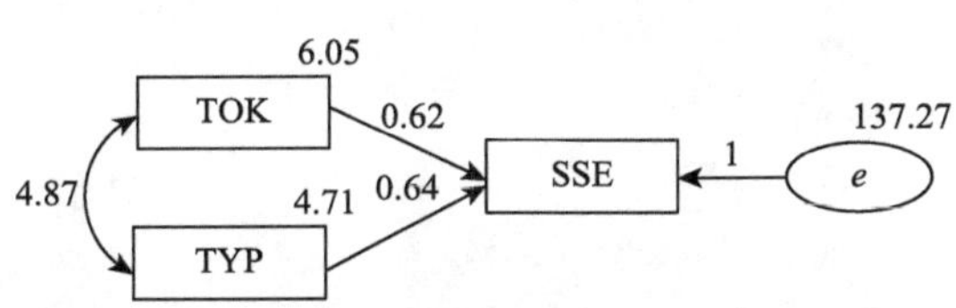

Figure 3.10 Unstandardized graphic output for a path model used for linear regression

In the standardized path diagram output, the correlation coefficients, standardized regression weights, and squared multiple correlation coefficients are all shown. In the unstandardized path diagram output, the covariances, unstandardized regression weights, and variances of the exogenous variables are all shown.

3.2.2 Comparison of Nested Path Analysis Models

Models developed by imposing parameter constraints on an old model are said to be nested in the old model. The new models and the old models are collectively called nested models. Nested models can be compared in the same analysis. By comparing nested models, we can decide whether it is plausible to impose the constraints. If a new model is no worse than the old one, we would prefer to use the new model, which is relatively simple. Now the application will be illustrated by the following examples.

3.2.2.1 Dataset and task

A group of students were required to rate the difficulties of a collection of passages to be used for reading comprehension exercises. The ratings for each passage were averaged, and used as an index of difficulty (DIF). The TTR (the number of types in every 100 running words), the number of words belonging to BASEWRD1 in every 100 running words (BAS1, as calculated by Range 32), and the ASL (as can be calculated by WordSmith Tools, Readability Analyzer or Syntactic Complexity Analyzer) for each passage were also computed. The data for 30 passages are shown in Table 3.4. We will employ the data to examine the usefulness of the TTR, BAS1 and ASL for the prediction of the DIF, and to test relevant hypotheses.

Table 3.4 Data for nested path analysis

Number	TTR	BAS1	ASL	DIF
1	40	61	30	1
2	43	68	28	2
3	47	65	27	1
4	51	76	24	3
5	52	70	23	4
6	53	79	23	3
7	55	79	22	3
8	55	77	23	4

Continued

Number	TTR	BAS1	ASL	DIF
9	56	80	27	5
10	56	80	26	5
11	57	71	24	5
12	57	80	25	4
13	57	81	25	5
14	58	85	24	6
15	59	69	23	6
16	59	71	23	6
17	59	79	22	6
18	59	77	22	7
19	60	83	23	6
20	60	81	22	6
21	61	84	22	6
22	62	85	21	7
23	64	86	21	7
24	66	87	21	9
25	69	86	20	7
26	72	78	18	8
27	74	79	19	8
28	75	79	20	8
29	77	81	17	7
30	80	87	14	9

3.2.2.2 Initial modeling and results

A. Modeling with the Amos Graphics

We have to start with a path diagram in which TTR, BAS1 and ASL are used to predict DIF (Figure 3.11). This is simply a path model with one variable regressing on three other variables.

Set the analysis properties as we do in Section 3.2.1.2, and the modeling is completed.

B. Estimation results

Run the analysis, and we will get the estimation results. Table 3.5 displays the text output from the analysis.

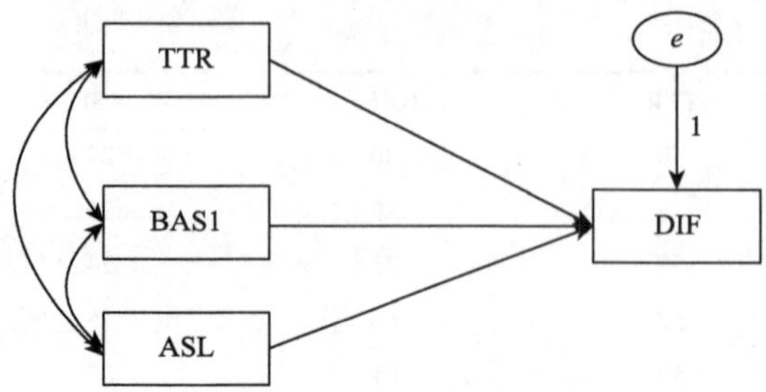

Figure 3.11　A path model with one variable predicted by three other variables

Table 3.5　Selected estimation results for a path model with one variable predicted by three other variables

Variables	Estimates	S.E.	C.R.	p
Regression weights				
DIF<---TTR	0.207	0.046	4.500	***
DIF<---BAS1	0.059	0.033	1.822	0.068
DIF<---ASL	0.085	0.125	0.679	0.497
Standardized regression weights				
DIF<---TTR	0.898			
DIF<---BAS1	0.184			
DIF<---ASL	0.129			

Based on the results, we can see that the regression weights of DIF on BAS1 and ASL are both insignificant (p>0.05).

3.2.2.3 Modeling with nested components

Here we will introduce the central issue of this section: nested path analysis models. Since the regression weights of DIF on BAS1 and ASL are both insignificant, we'll test our hypotheses that 1) the regression weight of DIF on BAS1 is zero; 2) the regression weight of DIF on ASL is zero; and 3) the regression weights of DIF on BAS1 and ASL are simultaneously zero. Following the steps below, we can test our hypotheses.

A. Adding labels for relevant parameters

Right-click the arrow pointing from BAS1 to DIF, and open the "Object Properties" dialogue box. Click the "Parameters" tab and type "*a*" in the "Regression weight" text box (Figure 3.12).

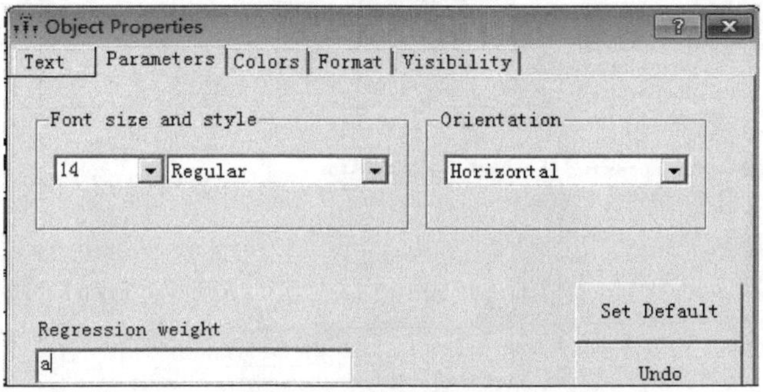

Figure 3.12 Adding labels for regressions weights to a model for nested path analysis

While keeping the dialogue box open, click on the arrow pointing from ASL to DIF and type "*b*" in the "Regression weight" box (the labels can be arbitrarily selected). Close the "Object Properties" dialogue box. Now you can see a path diagram with labels (Figure 3.13).

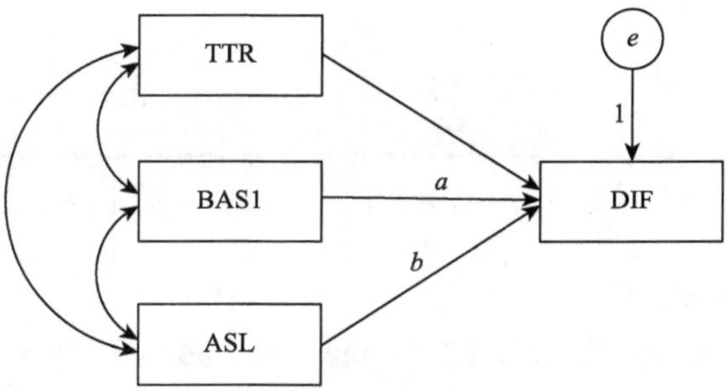

Figure 3.13 A path diagram for a model for nested path analysis

B. Managing Model A

a and *b* are labels for the regressions. Now we have four models to be compared: 1) a saturated model (Model A); 2) a model with $a = 0$ (Model B); 3) a model with $b = 0$ (Model C); 4) a model with $a = 0$ and $b = 0$ (Model D). To instruct Amos to compare those models, we have to manage the models in the succeeding procedure. Now we can begin with managing Model A.

Click "Analyze" and then "Manage Models", and open a dialogue box. Type "Model A" in the "Model Name" text box (Figure 3.14).

C. Managing Model B

Click "New" and type "Model B" as the name, and add "$a = 0$" in the "Parameter Constraints" box (Figure 3.15).

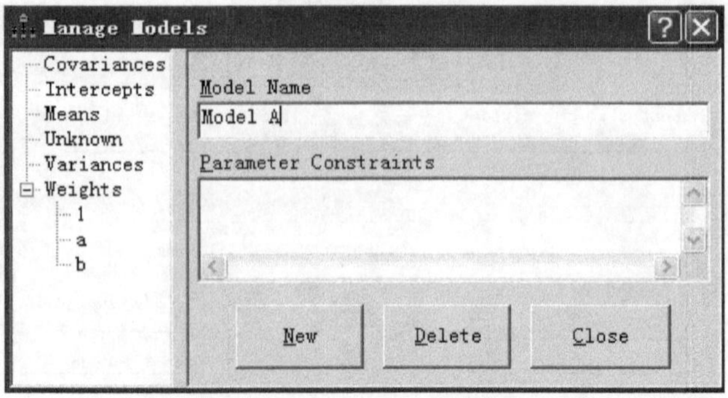

Figure 3.14　Specifying Model A to be used for nested path analysis

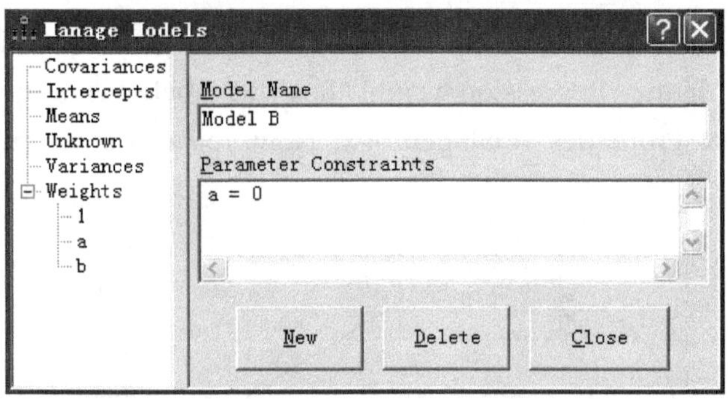

Figure 3.15　Specifying Model B to be used for nested path analysis

D. Managing Model C

Click "New" and type "Model C" for the name, and add "$b = 0$" in the "Parameter Constraints" box (Figure 3.16).

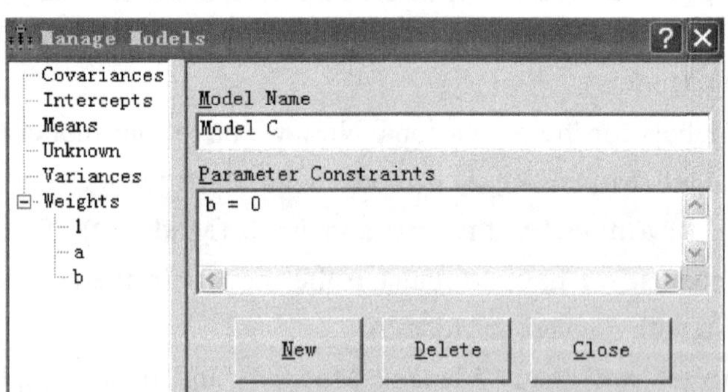

Figure 3.16　Specifying Model C to be used for nested path analysis

E. Managing Model D

Click "New" and enter "Model D" as the name, type "$a = 0$" and "$b = 0$"

simultaneously in the "Parameter Constraints" box. Close the box, run the analysis, and we can get the estimation results.

3.2.2.4 Text outputs for the nested models

Displayed in Table 3.6 and Table 3.7 are the text outputs for the analysis of the nested models. Sclcct "Model A", "Model B", "Model C" or "Model D" in the lower-left pane of the "Amos Output" window, and we can examine the results for each model.

Table 3.6 Summary for four models used in nested path analysis

Models	Variables	Values
Model A	Number of distinct sample moments	10
	Number of distinct parameters to be estimated	10
	df	0
	χ^2	0
	p	Cannot be computed
Model B	Number of distinct sample moments	10
	Number of distinct parameters to be estimated	9
	df	1
	χ^2	3.142
	p	0.076
Model C	Number of distinct sample moments	10
	Number of distinct parameters to be estimated	9
	df	1
	χ^2	0.458
	p	0.499
Model D	Number of distinct sample moments	10
	Number of distinct parameters to be estimated	8
	df	2
	χ^2	3.498
	p	0.174

Table 3.7 Comparison between the four models used in nested path analysis

Presupposition	Models	*df*	χ^2	*p*	NFI	IFI	RFI	TLI
Assuming Model A to be correct	Model B	1	3.142	0.076	0.026	0.026		
	Model C	1	0.458	0.499	0.004	0.004		
	Model D	2	3.498	0.174	0.029	0.029		
Assuming Model B to be correct	Model D	1	0.355	0.551	0.003	0.003	−0.070	−0.073
Assuming Model C to be correct	Model D	1	3.040	0.081	0.025	0.026	0.065	0.068

Model A is a saturated model. A saturated model always fits the data perfectly ($\chi^2 = 0$). Notes for Model B and Model C are similar. Each of the two models has one degree of freedom, which results from fixing one of the parameters at zero. Both models are acceptable ($p > 0.05$). Model D has two *df* values due to the two parameters fixed at zero. It is also acceptable.

In terms of simplicity, Model D is preferable to Model C and Model B, which are preferable to Model A.

But as the model becomes more and more simple, χ^2 becomes greater and greater. Both Model B and Model C have larger χ^2 than Model A; Model D still has a larger χ^2 than both Model B and Model C. A greater χ^2 means a larger discrepancy.

Is it plausible to use a simpler model at the cost of a better fit? The nested model comparisons suggest that 1) assuming Model A to be correct, Model B, Model C and Model D are not significantly worse (the differences are not statistically significant, as shown by the p values which are all greater than 0.05); 2) assuming Model B to be correct, Model D is not significantly worse ($p = 0.551 > 0.05$); 3) assuming Model C to be correct, Model D is not significantly worse ($p = 0.081 > 0.05$). In other words, it is plausible for us to use a simpler model even though the χ^2 is larger. Model D is preferable to any other models in the present example. There is no comparison between Model B and Model C, because they are both developed from (nested in) Model A with the addition of one constraint. In other words, they are equal in terms of simplicity. Needless to say, Model C is preferable to Model B, due to the smaller discrepancy function of χ^2. The NFI, IFI, RFI and TLI are all fit indexes (the larger, the better). The values displayed here are the differences between the nesting model and the nested one. For example, when Model B is nested in Model A, the NFI of Model A subtracted by the NFI of Model B equals 0.026. All those fit indexes are used to indicate how the goodness of fit changes as one or more constraints are imposed on a previous model.

3.2.2.5 Graphic output for the nested models

The output path diagrams for Model A, Model B, Model C and Model D are displayed in the following (Figure 3.17).

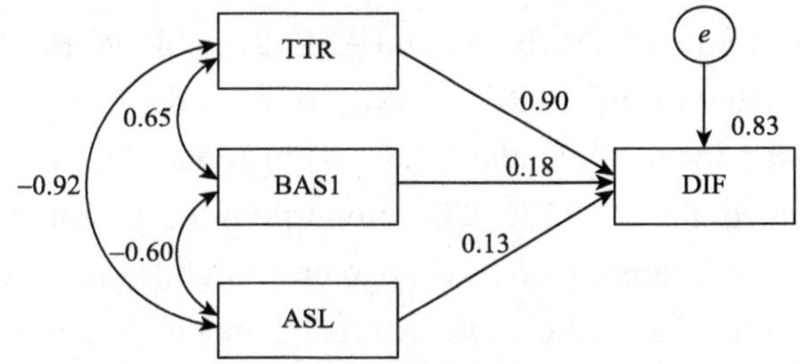

(a) Model A

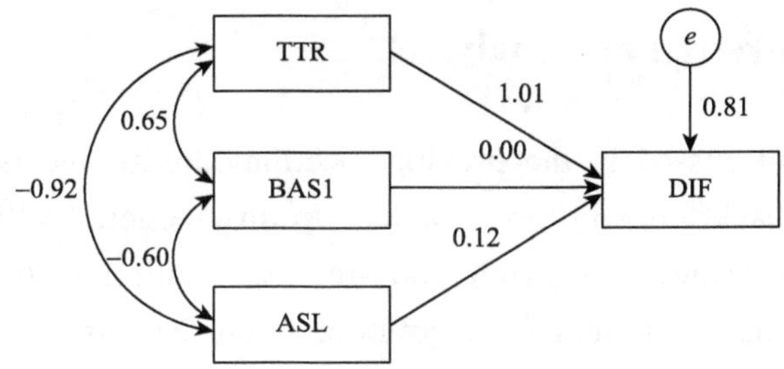

(b) Model B

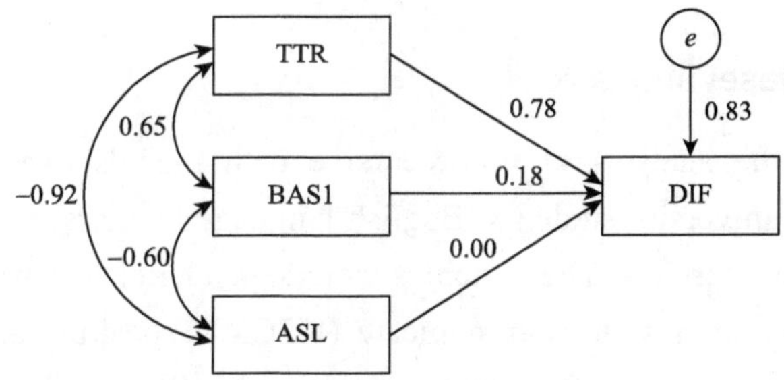

(c) Model C

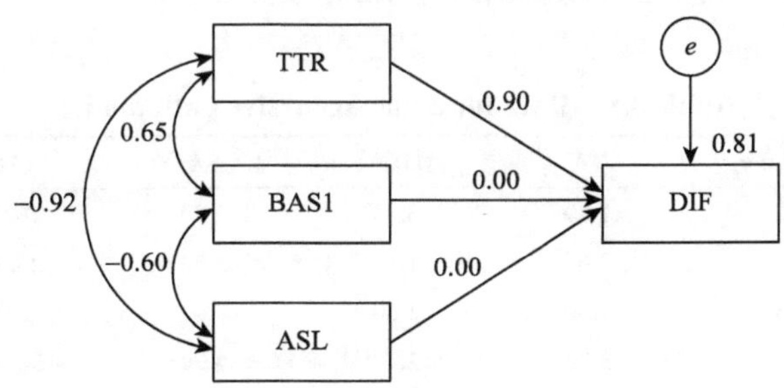

(d) Model D

Figure 3.17 Standardized path diagrams for models used in nested path analysis

From the path diagrams, we can see that 1) in Model A, 83% of the variance of

DIF can be accounted for by TTR, BAS1 and ASL; 2) in Model B, 81% of the variance of DIF can be accounted for by TTR and ASL; 3) in Model C, 83% of the variance of DIF can be accounted for by TTR and BAS1; 4) in Model D, 81% of the variance of DIF can be accounted for by TTR. The proportions of variance of the dependent variables explained by different models change only slightly, as are consistent with the results of model comparison (the more restricted model is not significantly worse assuming the less restricted one is correct).

3.2.3 Non-recursive Path Analysis

The models discussed in the previous sections are all recursive path models. There are no feedback loops in those models. In this section, we'll see models with feedback loops. Such models are called non-recursive path models. By tracing along the single-headed arrows in the path diagram of a non-recursive path model, we have the chance to arrive at the same variable. We will illustrate the application with the following example.

3.2.3.1 Dataset and task

To illustrate the analysis of non-recursive path models, we will use the data collected from 27 university students (English language learners) with a questionnaire and an English oral interview. The variables include gender (1 = female, 2 = male), trait anxiety (TA), unwillingness to communicate (UTCM), speaking anxiety (SA), TTR (the number of types in every 100 running words) and ASL calculated from the speech of each interviewee. The data are shown in Table 3.8.

Table 3.8 Data for a non-recursive path model

Number	Gender	TA	UTCM	SA	TTR	ASL
1	2	1.80	3.33	3.80	24.00	26.00
2	2	2.60	1.83	3.80	26.00	32.70
3	1	1.80	3.50	3.60	23.00	24.70
4	2	2.70	2.17	4.00	30.00	28.00
5	2	2.60	3.00	3.80	26.00	26.70
6	2	1.90	4.17	3.60	26.00	22.00
7	1	2.20	2.83	3.20	31.00	36.70
8	2	1.80	3.33	4.00	30.00	23.30
9	2	3.10	3.00	2.80	37.00	32.70

Continued

Number	Gender	TA	UTCM	SA	TTR	ASL
10	2	2.20	2.50	3.60	26.00	22.70
11	1	1.90	3.00	3.60	27.00	30.70
12	2	2.40	2.17	3.40	30.00	30.70
13	2	2.30	2.00	3.40	31.00	22.70
14	2	2.30	3.33	3.40	24.00	21.30
15	2	1.80	2.83	3.60	32.00	24.00
16	1	2.50	2.17	3.40	28.00	28.70
17	2	1.80	3.00	4.40	26.00	25.30
18	2	1.40	2.67	3.80	31.00	32.70
19	2	3.00	2.83	3.60	29.00	27.30
20	2	2.40	2.83	3.60	27.00	25.30
21	2	2.70	1.83	3.40	36.00	40.70
22	2	3.30	1.17	4.20	25.00	24.70
23	2	2.20	3.33	3.60	33.00	25.30
24	1	3.20	3.00	3.60	32.00	33.30
25	1	2.30	2.33	2.40	25.00	26.70
26	1	1.80	3.17	3.40	20.00	22.70
27	2	1.90	2.67	3.00	13.00	32.70

Based on experience, the author developed the following model and wanted to examine whether the data supported the model (Figure 3.18).

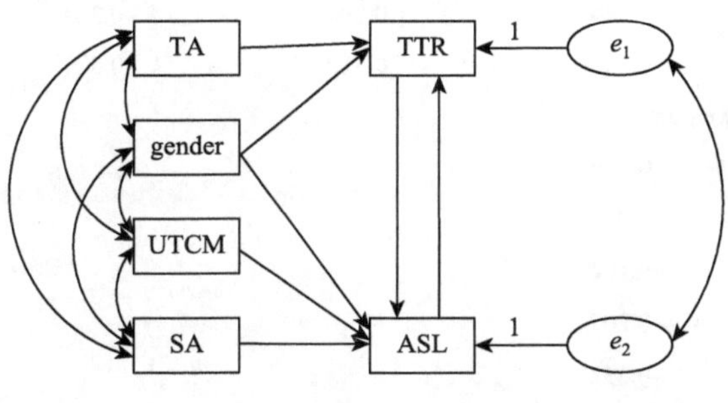

Figure 3.18 Input path diagram for a non-recursive path model

This is a non-recursive path model. TTR and ASL are supposed to have mutual influence. You may have noticed that the error terms e_1 and e_2 are correlated. In recursive models, error terms are independent by default. In a non-recursive path model, error terms are generally assumed to be correlated if they are related to variables in a feedback loop.

3.2.3.2 Estimation results

To test the model, we have to draw a path diagram like Figure 3.18, and run the analysis. The text results corresponding to the model are shown in Table 3.9 and Table 3.10.

Table 3.9 Summary for a non-recursive path model

Variables	Values
Number of distinct sample moments	21
Number of distinct parameters to be estimated	20
df	1
χ^2	0.026
p	0.871
Stability index for ASL and TTR	0.043

Table 3.10 Selected estimation results for a non-recursive path model

Variables	Estimates	S.E.	C.R.	*p*
Regression weights				
TTR<---TA	3.773	2.534	1.489	0.136
TTR<---gender	1.026	2.400	0.427	0.669
ASL<---gender	−1.771	2.065	−0.858	0.391
ASL<---SA	−2.504	2.103	−1.191	0.234
ASL<---UTCM	−2.558	1.374	−1.861	0.063
TTR<---ASL	−0.144	0.590	−0.244	0.807
ASL<---TTR	0.296	0.519	0.570	0.569
Standardized regression weights				
TTR<---TA	0.379			
TTR<---gender	0.093			
ASL<---gender	−0.162			
ASL<---SA	−0.207			
ASL<---UTCM	−0.332			
TTR<---ASL	−0.144			
ASL<---TTR	0.297			
Covariances				
TA<-->gender	0.013	0.042	0.310	0.757
TA<-->UTCM	−0.148	0.066	−2.253	0.024
TA<-->SA	−0.015	0.038	−0.400	0.689
gender<-->UTCM	−0.030	0.054	−0.563	0.574

Continued

Variables	Estimates	S.E.	C.R.	*p*
gender<-->SA	0.063	0.036	1.723	0.085
UTCM<-->SA	−0.004	0.049	−0.082	0.935
e_1<-->e_2	2.910	14.472	0.201	0.841
Correlations				
TA<-->gender	0.061			
TA<-->UTCM	−0.493			
TA<-->SA	−0.079			
gender<-->UTCM	−0.111			
gender<-->SA	0.359			
UTCM<-->SA	−0.016			
e_1<-->e_2	0.154			
Variances				
TA	0.234	0.065	3.606	***
gender	0.192	0.053	3.606	***
UTCM	0.387	0.107	3.606	***
SA	0.158	0.044	3.606	***
e_1	22.272	12.403	1.796	0.073
e_2	16.074	4.497	3.574	***
Squared multiple correlations				
ASL	0.302			
TTR	0.039			

This model has 6 observed variables. The total number of distinct sample moments is 21. The total number of distinct parameters to be estimated is 20, including 6 variances, 7 covariances and 7 regression weights. The *df* is 21 − 20 = 1. With χ^2 = 0.026 (p = 0.871), the model is acceptable.

A stability index is calculated for every feedback loop in a non-recursive path model. When all the stability indexes in a model are smaller than 1, the system of linear dependencies is considered to be stable. Otherwise, it is unstable, which implies that the model is incorrect or that the size of the sample is too small. The stability index here is 0.043, which suggests that the model is stable.

The ASL and TTR are involved in the feedback loop. The two variables have a mutual influence.

The estimates of the parameters reveal that none of regression weights is statistically significant. The squared multiple correlation shows that 30.2% of the variance of ASL and 3.9% of the variance of TTR can be accounted for by the relevant predictors. The model is complex but not so useful, especially for the prediction of TTR. Below is the standardized output path diagram (Figure 3.19).

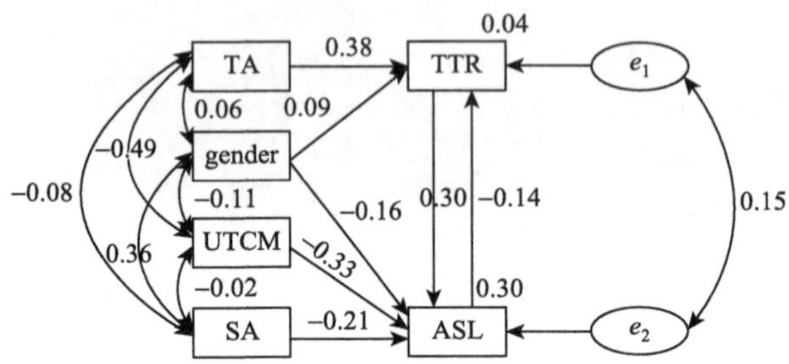

Figure 3.19 Standardized output path diagram for a non-recursive model

3.2.4 Multiple Group Path Analysis

With SEM, we can not only evaluate the fit of different models for the same set of data, but also evaluate the fit of a single model for different groups. There are two methods to fit the same model to different groups: to perform separate analyses, or to fit the model to different groups in one analysis. The second method has advantages over the first one. It can not only test the significance of the difference found between the groups, but also provide more accurate parameter estimates. The application is illustrated with the example below.

3.2.4.1 Dataset and task

This example involves a sample of 212 university students, with 113 boys and 99 girls. The writing self-efficiency (WSE), speaking self-efficiency (SSE), writing anxiety (WA), SA, writing information density (WID = the number of content words in every 100 running words in each writing), and speaking information density (SID = the number of content words in every 100 running words in each speech) of all the participants were investigated. WSE, SSE, WA and SA are investigated by a questionnaire, while WID and SID are analyzed with Tree Tagger and AntConc. The data are displayed in Table 3.11.

Table 3.11 Data for a multiple group path analysis

Number	Gender	WSE	SSE	WA	SA	WID	SID
1	1	39	30	31	35	68	81
2	1	45	30	31	21	71	80
3	1	31	37	34	20	70	78
4	1	48	29	45	31	67	78
5	1	37	29	50	32	67	77
6	2	43	43	58	29	67	77
7	1	42	35	30	27	70	75
8	1	38	29	30	28	70	75
9	2	40	43	54	34	68	75
10	2	44	45	61	24	68	75
11	2	43	32	40	30	67	75
12	2	45	33	42	22	68	74
13	2	42	40	60	35	67	74
14	1	34	28	64	33	66	74
15	2	45	42	46	19	70	73
16	1	36	35	32	19	69	73
17	1	36	45	32	19	69	73
18	2	47	34	44	20	69	73
19	1	34	30	39	31	68	73
20	2	38	42	41	23	67	73
21	1	37	31	53	32	68	72
22	2	41	41	56	28	67	72
23	2	37	40	39	26	67	72
24	2	38	41	52	33	67	72
25	1	36	31	49	36	66	72
26	1	33	32	55	37	69	71
27	1	28	41	29	18	69	71
28	1	33	32	39	38	68	71
29	1	34	29	47	34	67	71
30	2	41	38	58	33	67	71
31	1	32	33	30	35	65	71
32	1	63	31	41	33	70	70
33	1	28	35	35	32	69	70
34	2	43	40	45	19	69	70
35	1	36	32	42	36	68	70
36	1	44	34	44	21	68	70

Continued

Number	Gender	WSE	SSE	WA	SA	WID	SID
37	2	44	41	65	37	67	70
38	2	39	40	54	27	66	70
39	2	29	40	65	34	66	70
40	2	44	28	51	38	67	69
41	2	37	40	51	31	66	69
42	1	41	45	45	28	69	68
43	1	31	38	49	42	69	68
44	2	39	38	41	23	69	68
45	1	31	30	50	33	68	68
46	1	32	29	69	37	67	68
47	1	33	28	58	33	67	68
48	2	45	42	67	39	67	68
49	1	29	30	39	32	69	67
50	2	41	38	43	39	69	67
51	2	41	39	42	25	69	67
52	2	43	36	48	36	69	67
53	1	32	29	61	39	68	67
54	2	40	44	42	28	68	67
55	1	35	29	63	30	67	67
56	1	39	28	41	29	67	67
57	2	36	33	59	33	66	67
58	1	37	25	49	25	71	66
59	1	31	30	69	35	68	66
60	1	26	32	27	17	68	66
61	1	31	30	69	36	67	66
62	2	42	34	47	31	67	66
63	2	43	27	51	37	67	66
64	2	39	37	55	33	66	66
65	2	35	38	48	30	66	66
66	2	33	39	56	37	66	66
67	2	33	39	60	28	65	66
68	1	26	38	39	47	68	65
69	1	48	39	39	21	68	65
70	1	34	30	72	34	67	65
71	1	37	32	35	35	67	65
72	1	31	27	66	36	67	65

Continued

Number	Gender	WSE	SSE	WA	SA	WID	SID
73	2	38	38	66	41	67	65
74	2	37	36	55	31	66	65
75	2	34	41	63	34	65	65
76	1	39	43	68	43	68	64
77	1	29	46	74	39	68	64
78	1	29	29	73	39	67	64
79	1	34	28	61	29	66	64
80	2	40	34	57	41	66	64
81	2	27	37	60	31	65	64
82	1	46	24	46	24	70	63
83	1	30	28	70	37	67	63
84	1	37	27	63	28	67	63
85	1	30	29	66	34	67	63
86	1	30	29	66	33	67	63
87	2	32	37	54	35	66	63
88	1	25	36	38	45	68	62
89	1	33	29	69	33	66	62
90	2	42	37	62	36	66	62
91	2	37	36	39	28	68	61
92	2	43	37	62	54	68	61
93	1	37	41	65	41	67	61
94	1	28	44	71	38	67	61
95	1	28	27	70	37	67	61
96	2	47	37	76	40	64	61
97	2	31	30	67	43	63	61
98	1	29	26	67	36	67	60
99	2	39	37	64	44	67	60
100	1	36	26	61	27	66	60
101	2	39	25	47	34	66	60
102	2	37	37	64	40	66	60
103	2	35	42	65	31	66	60
104	2	31	36	52	34	65	60
105	2	45	36	51	39	68	59
106	2	42	36	60	52	67	59
107	2	35	36	62	38	66	59
108	2	40	37	60	35	66	59

Continued

Number	Gender	WSE	SSE	WA	SA	WID	SID
109	2	30	31	65	42	63	59
110	2	37	35	62	42	67	58
111	1	29	23	53	25	64	58
112	2	45	35	70	39	63	58
113	2	44	35	49	38	67	57
114	2	37	35	62	44	67	56
115	2	34	34	59	37	65	56
116	1	48	25	44	55	70	55
117	2	40	34	45	34	68	55
118	2	36	34	59	41	66	55
119	2	42	35	46	23	68	54
120	2	48	33	45	22	68	54
121	2	33	33	53	46	64	54
122	1	27	21	50	23	63	54
123	2	43	34	67	37	63	54
124	2	44	30	42	36	67	53
125	2	41	27	49	35	66	53
126	2	38	33	55	48	66	53
127	2	28	39	63	34	65	53
128	2	27	27	60	39	62	53
129	2	24	34	80	45	60	53
130	2	35	33	57	39	65	52
131	2	35	32	57	40	65	52
132	1	65	24	42	52	69	51
133	2	40	32	45	35	66	51
134	1	26	20	48	22	62	51
135	2	23	32	77	44	60	51
136	2	38	32	43	40	67	50
137	2	31	32	51	44	64	50
138	2	31	30	67	44	64	50
139	1	43	23	40	50	68	49
140	2	33	32	73	48	64	49
141	2	27	40	73	48	62	49
142	2	22	31	74	42	59	49
143	2	46	32	44	46	68	48
144	1	24	21	51	28	63	48

Continued

Number	Gender	WSE	SSE	WA	SA	WID	SID
145	2	30	31	49	42	63	48
146	2	32	31	70	46	64	47
147	2	26	38	70	46	61	47
148	1	23	23	51	26	64	46
149	1	23	23	51	26	63	46
150	1	25	23	53	25	63	46
151	2	28	28	62	40	62	46
152	1	22	20	48	26	63	45
153	2	25	36	67	44	61	45
154	2	42	29	40	42	66	43
155	1	22	21	48	25	63	43
156	1	22	21	48	24	63	43
157	1	24	21	50	24	62	43
158	2	36	35	66	42	66	42
159	2	37	37	69	43	66	42
160	2	34	34	64	39	65	42
161	1	22	19	46	25	62	42
162	1	21	20	46	24	62	41
163	1	21	20	46	23	62	41
164	1	41	30	107	64	69	40
165	1	37	34	82	59	62	40
166	1	23	20	48	23	62	40
167	1	34	35	74	53	61	40
168	1	19	17	114	52	57	40
169	2	33	33	61	38	65	39
170	1	22	23	44	33	63	39
171	1	45	27	41	55	70	38
172	1	35	36	77	56	62	37
173	1	21	22	42	31	62	36
174	1	21	19	126	57	57	36
175	1	42	26	39	52	69	35
176	2	24	25	61	42	58	35
177	1	20	21	40	30	62	34
178	2	23	23	59	41	58	34
179	1	40	25	38	50	68	33
180	1	20	18	119	54	57	33

Continued

Number	Gender	WSE	SSE	WA	SA	WID	SID
181	2	22	23	57	57	57	32
182	2	21	21	54	38	57	32
183	1	29	14	93	59	62	29
184	2	27	27	89	60	61	28
185	1	22	24	104	63	58	28
186	1	27	13	88	56	61	27
187	1	26	13	84	54	61	26
188	2	26	26	86	50	61	26
189	1	22	24	123	58	58	26
190	1	18	23	99	60	57	26
191	1	24	18	96	62	60	25
192	2	25	25	72	53	60	25
193	1	17	24	95	57	57	25
194	2	24	24	79	53	60	24
195	1	21	23	116	57	57	24
196	1	27	20	106	69	61	23
197	1	20	22	111	52	57	23
198	1	43	32	113	68	70	22
199	1	25	19	100	65	60	21
200	1	30	24	99	65	59	21
201	1	39	29	102	61	69	19
202	1	28	21	93	73	59	19
203	1	27	20	89	59	58	18
204	1	10	19	109	73	57	18
205	1	18	15	102	59	59	17
206	1	9	18	103	76	57	16
207	1	17	14	96	56	58	15
208	1	9	17	98	63	57	15
209	1	16	14	92	53	58	14
210	1	30	23	79	43	65	12
211	1	29	21	75	45	64	11
212	1	28	20	72	43	64	10

Note: In the gender column, 1 = boy, and 2 = girl

Based on the dataset, a path model has been built, which is to be simultaneously tested on both gender groups (Figure 3.20).

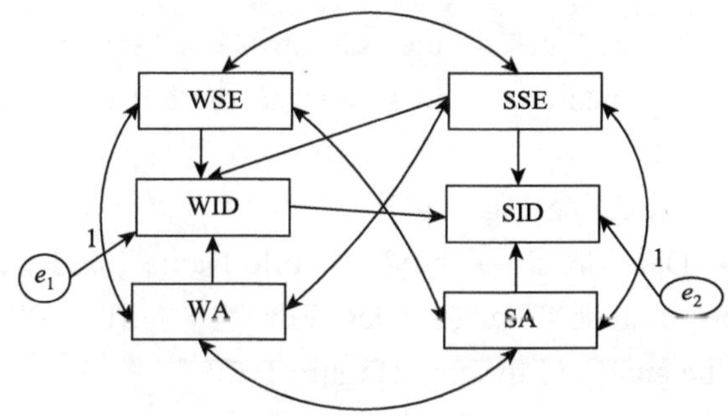

Figure 3.20 A path model to be tested on multiple groups

We will now examine 1) whether the boy group and the girl group can share the model displayed here, and 2) whether the boy group and the girl group can share the parameters if they can share the same model.

When an analysis involves different groups, the group data can be saved in the same file or in different files. In this example, all the data are saved in a single file, with the variable genders indicating the group membership (1 = boy; 2 = girl).

3.2.4.2 Creating the model shared by girls and boys

Two stages (Stage One and Stage Two) are involved in the analysis. In Stage One, we have to produce a path diagram like Figure 3.20, and examine whether the girl group and the boy group can share the model. To instruct Amos to analyze different groups, we have to perform the following tasks.

A. Naming the groups

Click “Analyze” and then “Manage Groups”. In the “Group Name” text box, enter “boy” (Figure 3.21).

Figure 3.21 Naming the boy group for a path model for multiple groups

Click “New”, and type “girl” in the “Group Name” text box. Click “Close” and you will see the group names appear in a panel to the left of the drawing area of the Amos Graphics window.

B. Importing the file for each group

Click “File” → “Data Files” → “boy” → “File Name”, and we can select the file to be analyzed for boys; click “File” → “Data Files” → “girl” → “File Name”, and we can select the file to be analyzed for girls (Figure 3.22).

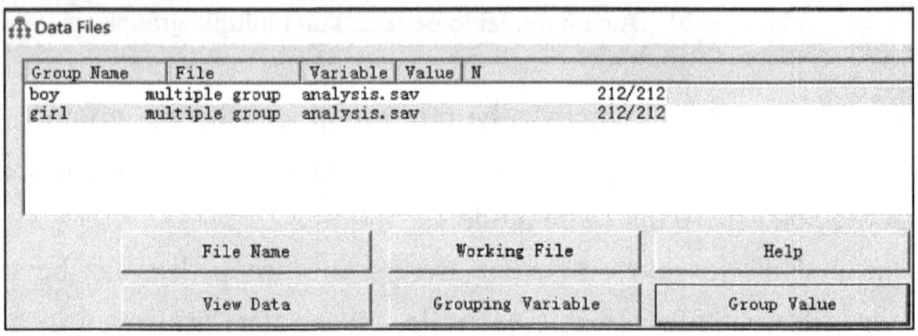

Figure 3.22 Importing the data file for a path model for multiple groups

C. Choosing a grouping variable for the boy group

Click “boy” and then “Grouping Variable”, select “gender” as the grouping variable, and click “OK” (Figure 3.23).

D. Choosing the group value for the boy group

Now click “Group Value”, select “1” as the group value, and click “OK” (Figure 3.24).

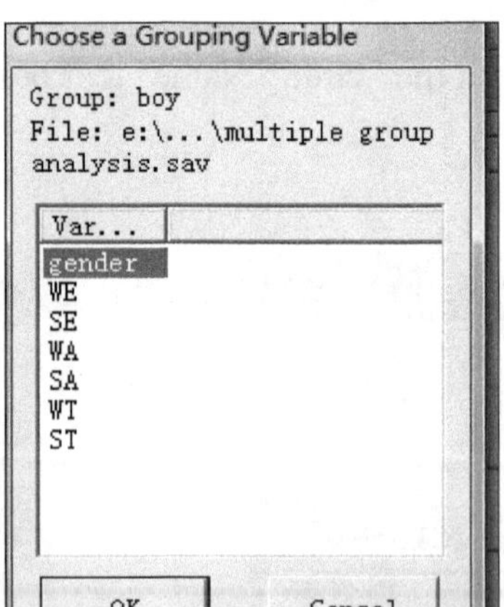

Figure 3.23 Selecting “gender” as the grouping variable for the boy group

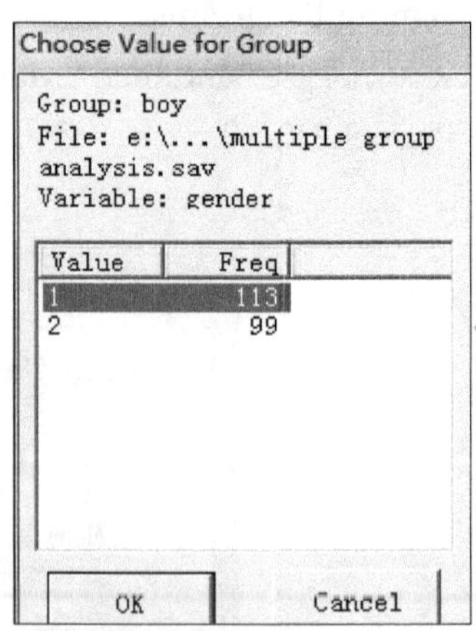

Figure 3.24 Selecting “1” as the grouping value for the boy group

E. Specifying the grouping variable and group value for the girl group

Through a similar procedure, specify the grouping variable and group value for girls. When the specification is completed, the "Data Files" dialogue box should be like as follows (Figure 3.25).

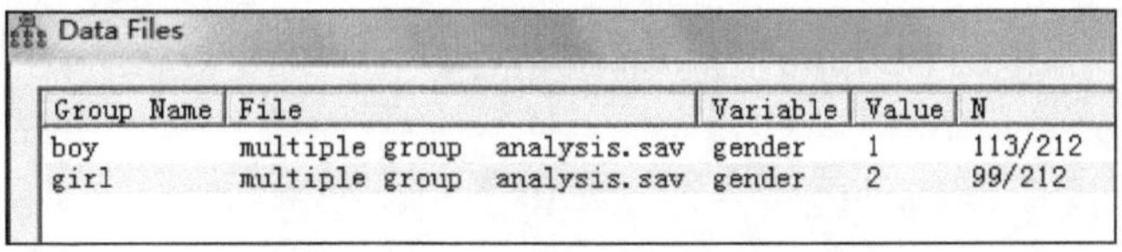

Figure 3.25 A competed data specification for a path model for multiple groups

Close the "Data Files" dialogue box and run the analysis.

3.2.4.3 Text output for the shared model

The selected text output for the shared model is displayed in Table 3.12 and Table 3.13. We have to focus on the fitness of the model.

Table 3.12 Summary for a path model for multiple groups

Variables	Values
Number of distinct sample moments	42
Number of distinct parameters to be estimated	36
df	6
χ^2	6.410
p	0.379

Table 3.13 Selected estimation results for a path model for multiple groups

Variables	Estimates	S.E.	C.R.	*p*
Regression weights (boy)				
WID<---WSE	0.194	0.023	8.458	***
WID<---SSE	0.171	0.029	5.803	***
WID<---WA	−0.059	0.008	−7.262	***
SID<---WID	1.611	0.328	4.911	***
SID<---SSE	0.857	0.174	4.941	***
SID<---SA	−0.588	0.072	−8.143	***
Standardized regression weights (boy)				
WID<---WSE	0.442			
WID<---SSE	0.300			

Continued

Variables	Estimates	S.E.	C.R.	*p*
WID<---WA	–0.366			
SID<---WID	0.332			
SID<---SSE	0.310			
SID<---SA	–0.431			
Covariances (boy)				
WSE<-->WA	–108.591	25.118	–4.323	***
WSE<-->SSE	33.953	7.247	4.685	***
SSE<-->SA	–36.423	10.728	–3.395	***
WA<-->SA	296.579	45.511	6.517	***
WSE<-->SA	–30.254	13.460	–2.248	0.025
WA<-->SSE	–80.685	19.282	–4.184	***
Correlations (boy)				
WSE<-->WA	–0.448			
WSE<-->SSE	0.494			
SSE<-->SA	–0.339			
WA<-->SA	0.782			
WSE<-->SA	–0.217			
WA<-->SSE	–0.431			
Variances (boy)				
WSE	88.981	11.894	7.481	***
WA	661.129	88.373	7.481	***
SSE	53.102	7.098	7.481	***
SA	217.627	29.090	7.481	***
e_1	3.614	0.483	7.481	***
e_2	97.160	12.987	7.481	***
Squared multiple correlations (boy)				
WID	0.790			
SID	0.760			
Regression weights (girl)				
WID<---WSE	0.233	0.022	10.787	***
WID<---SSE	0.183	0.025	7.356	***
WID<---WA	–0.069	0.012	–5.615	***
SID<---WID	1.354	0.325	4.165	***
SID<---SSE	0.875	0.165	5.302	***

Continued

Variables	Estimates	S.E.	C.R.	p
SID<---SA	−0.477	0.101	−4.709	***
Standardized regression weights (girl)				
WID<---WSE	0.562			
WID<---SSE	0.331			
WID<---WA	−0.267			
SID<---WID	0.313			
SID<---SSE	0.366			
SID<---SA	−0.324			
Covariances (girl)				
WSE<-->WA	−38.832	8.496	−4.570	***
WSE<-->SSE	15.245	3.869	3.940	***
SSE<-->SA	−21.684	4.838	−4.482	***
WA<-->SA	57.304	10.836	5.288	***
WSE<-->SA	−28.006	6.426	−4.358	***
WA<-->SSE	−8.187	5.696	−1.437	0.151
Correlations (girl)				
WSE<-->WA	−0.520			
WSE<-->SSE	0.434			
SSE<-->SA	−0.508			
WA<-->SA	0.632			
WSE<-->SA	−0.490			
WA<-->SSE	−0.147			
Variances (girl)				
WSE	47.012	6.714	7.002	***
WA	118.512	16.925	7.002	***
SSE	26.286	3.754	7.002	***
SA	69.451	9.918	7.002	***
e_1	1.285	0.183	7.002	***
e_2	41.813	5.971	7.002	***
Squared multiple correlations (girl)				
WID	0.840			
SID	0.722			

In analysis with more than one group, the total number of moments is the sum of moments in each group, so is the total number of parameters. In each group, there are 6 observed variables. The number of moments for each group is $6(6+1)/2=21$. The total number of moments for both the girl group and the boy group is 42.

There are 18 parameters for each group (6 variances, 6 covariances, and 6 regression weights); therefore, the total number of parameters is 36. With $\chi^2=6.410$, and $p=0.379>0.05$, the model is acceptable. This means that the boy group and the girl group can share the same model.

3.2.4.4 Examining the model with parameters shared by girls and boys

Though boys and girls can share the same model, the parameter estimates are not the same. For example, the regression of WID on WSE is 0.194 for boys, and 0.233 for girls; the covariance between SSE and WSE is 33.953 for boys, and 15.245 for girls. Are the differences in the corresponding parameters statistically significant? To answer the question, we have to modify the model: Assign a label to each parameter, and specify each label to be shared by different groups. If the new model is acceptable, we can conclude that the parameters can be shared by different groups. In other words, the differences in parameters are not significant. There are 18 parameters in each model. For the illustration purpose, we will only examine whether the 6 covariances and the 6 regression weights can be shared.

A. Modeling with Amos Graphics

Begin with the model specified in Stage One. Right-click a single- or double-headed arrow in the path diagram of the model and open the "Object Properties" dialogue box. Click the "Parameters" tab and type an arbitrary label name (such as a, b, c...) in the "Regression weight" or the "Covariance" text box. Select "All groups" to tell Amos that all groups will share the label (Figure 3.26).

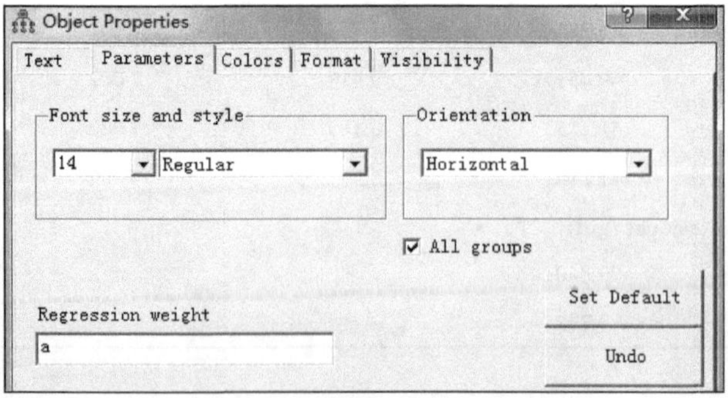

Figure 3.26 Specifying a shared regression weight for a path model for multiple groups

Repeat the procedure, until all of the single- or double-headed arrows have shared labels. Each time a label is typed, remember to select "All groups". After all labels are assigned, close the "Object Properties" dialogue box. The model should look like as follows (Figure 3.27).

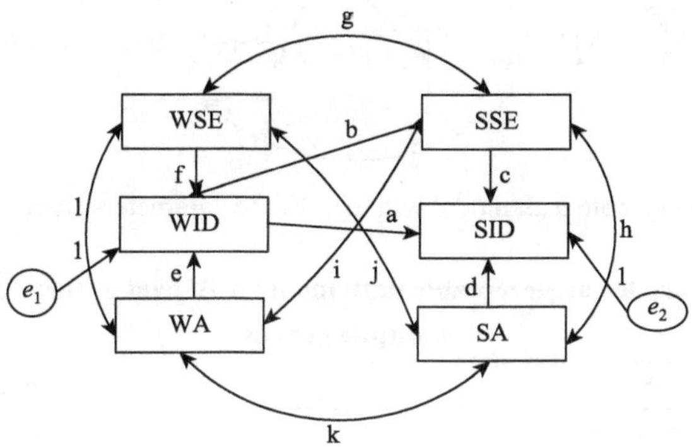

Figure 3.27 A path model with parameter labels shared by multiple groups

B. Examining the text output for the model with shared parameters

The summary text output for the model with shared parameters (regression weights and covariances) is as follows (Table 3.14).

Table 3.14 Summary for a path model with parameter labels shared by multiple groups

Variables	Values
Number of distinct sample moments	42
Number of distinct parameters to be estimated	24
df	18
χ^2	97.776
p	0.000

The $p = 0.000$ suggests that boys and girls cannot share all the regression weights and covariances.

3.2.4.5 Modifying the shared model parameters and examining the output

Since all the regression weights and covariances cannot be shared simultaneously, we have to refer to the M.I. and modify the model. After the modification and analysis, we can get a model with a few shared parameters as shown in Figure 3.28. This model is acceptable. The relevant text output is presented in Table 3.15 and Table 3.16.

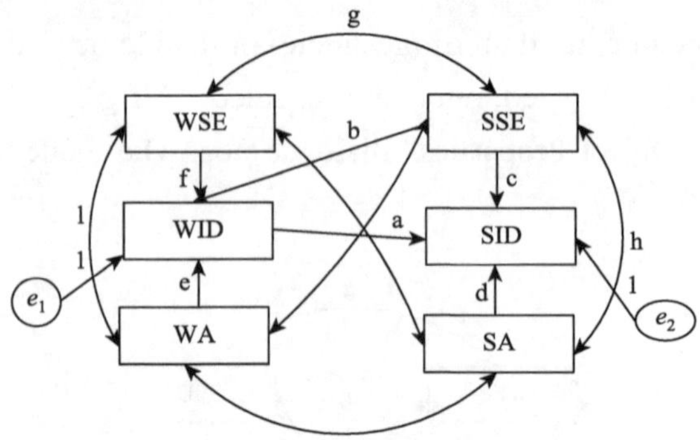

Figure 3.28 An acceptable path model with part of the parameters shared by multiple groups

Table 3.15 Summary for an acceptable path model with part of the parameters shared by multiple groups

Variables	Values
Number of distinct sample moments	42
Number of distinct parameters to be estimated	27
df	15
χ^2	24.237
p	0.061

Table 3.16 Selected estimation results for an acceptable path model with part of the parameters shared by multiple groups

Variables	Estimates	S.E.	C.R.	*p*
Regression weights (boy)				
WID<---WSE	0.221	0.015	15.026	***
WID<---SSE	0.175	0.019	9.245	***
WID<---WA	−0.060	0.007	−9.098	***
SID<---WID	1.471	0.227	6.468	***
SID<---SSE	0.856	0.119	7.171	***
SID<---SA	−0.550	0.057	−9.594	***
Standardized regression weights (boy)				
WID<---WSE	0.490			
WID<---SSE	0.306			
WID<---WA	−0.373			
SID<---WID	0.315			
SID<---SSE	0.321			
SID<---SA	−0.438			
Covariances (boy)				
WSE<-->WA	−54.931	9.415	−5.834	***
WSE<-->SSE	21.990	3.638	6.044	***

Continued

Variables	Estimates	S.E.	C.R.	p
SSE<-->SA	−27.828	4.624	−6.018	***
WA<-->SA	273.847	38.949	7.031	***
WSE<-->SA	−6.593	8.660	−0.761	0.446
WA<-->SSE	−57.897	11.756	−4.925	***
Correlations (boy)				
WSE<-->WA	−0.260			
WSE<-->SSE	0.368			
SSE<-->SA	−0.278			
WA<-->SA	0.775			
WSE<-->SA	−0.052			
WA<-->SSE	−0.348			
Regression weights (girl)				
WID<---WSE	0.221	0.015	15.026	***
WID<---SSE	0.175	0.019	9.245	***
WID<---WA	−0.060	0.007	−9.098	***
SID<---WID	1.471	0.227	6.468	***
SID<---SSE	0.856	0.119	7.171	***
SID<---SA	−0.550	0.057	−9.594	***
Standardized regression weights (girl)				
WID<---WSE	0.562			
WID<---SSE	0.316			
WID<---WA	−0.235			
SID<---WID	0.321			
SID<---SSE	0.338			
SID<---SA	−0.356			
Covariances (girl)				
WSE<-->WA	−54.931	9.415	−5.834	***
WSE<-->SSE	21.990	3.638	6.044	***
SSE<-->SA	−27.828	4.624	−6.018	***
WA<-->SA	71.762	12.002	5.979	***
WSE<-->SA	−39.865	6.991	−5.703	***
WA<-->SSE	−16.422	5.907	−2.780	0.005
Correlations (girl)				
WSE<-->WA	−0.609			
WSE<-->SSE	0.525			
SSE<-->SA	−0.570			
WA<-->SA	0.682			
WSE<-->SA	−0.580			
WA<-->SSE	−0.256			

Based on the results, we can draw the conclusion that 1) the boy group and the girl group can share the same model, and 2) the boy group and the girl group can share all the regression weights and some of the covariances.

In Table 3.11, you may have noticed that although the shared regression weights and covariances are the same for the boy group and the girl group, the standardized regression weights and correlations are not the same. This is because of the different corresponding standard deviations. The graphic outputs for the boy group and the girl group are shown in Figure 3.29 and Figure 3.30.

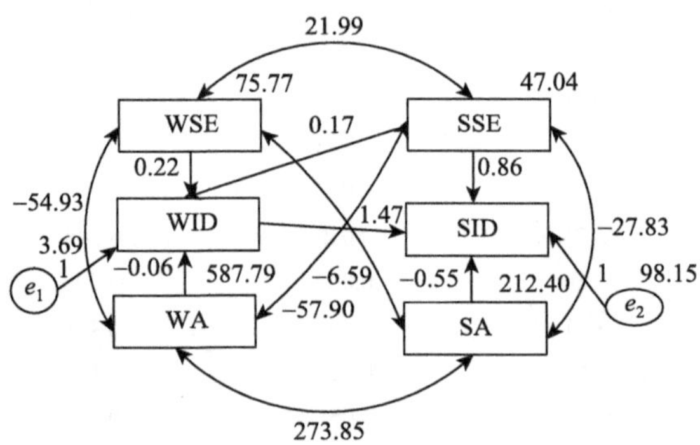

Figure 3.29 An unstandardized output path diagram for the boy group

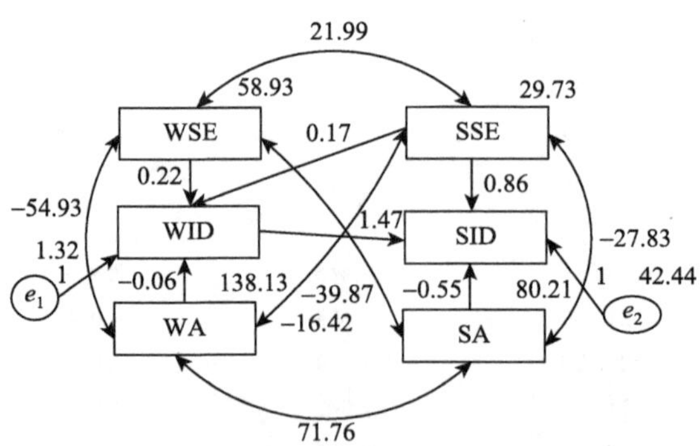

Figure 3.30 An unstandardized output path diagram for the girl group

3.3 Summary

Path models examine the relationships among observed variables. Recursive path models have no feedback loops. No variables have effects on each other. The variables being predicted are called endogenous variables. Each endogenous variable has an error variable, suggesting that its variation depends not only on the known predictors, but also on unknown factors represented by the error variables. Nonrecursive path models have feedback loops, indicating mutual influences existing between variables. The error variables corresponding to variables in a feedback loop are usually assumed to be correlated. In path analysis, we can not only compare the fit of different models simultaneously, but also decide whether different groups can share the same model or certain parameters of that model.

Chapter 4 Factor Analysis Models and Structural Regression Models

Factor analysis models and structural regression models are more complicated than path analysis models. In fact, they are developed from path analysis models, and can be used to test more complex hypotheses.

4.1 Factor Analysis Models

Factors are unobserved variables or latent variables. Factor analysis is a statistical technique in which one or more factors are used to explain the relationships among a group of observed variables. The observed variables explained by a factor are called indicators of the factor. The regression weight of an indicator on the factor is called factor loading. As dependent (endogenous) variables, indicators are assumed to be partly explained by the corresponding factors and partly by unknown variables (error terms).

4.1.1 Types of Elementary Factor Analysis Models

4.1.1.1 Confirmative factor analysis models

The factor analysis is called confirmative factor analysis (CFA) when the purpose is to test whether a pre-existing number of factors are capable of explaining the relationships among the observed variables. There are four sub-types of CFA.

A. Different indicators having loadings on a common factor

Such models have one common factor and at least three indicators. In the path diagram, the common factor sends out a single-headed arrow to each indicator, which simultaneously receives a single-headed arrow from an error variable. The following is an example, in which variable_1, variable_2 and variable_3 are assumed to have loadings on the common factor F (Figure 4.1).

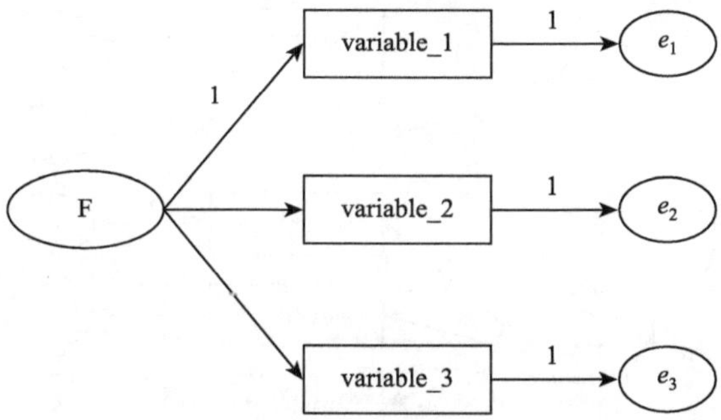

Figure 4.1 Different clusters of indicators having loadings on a common factor

B. Different indicators having loadings on different factors

The following is an example of factor analysis models, in which variable_1 and variable_2 are assumed to have loadings on a common factor F_1, and variable_3 and variable_4 are hypothesized to have loadings on another common factor F_2 (Figure 4.2).

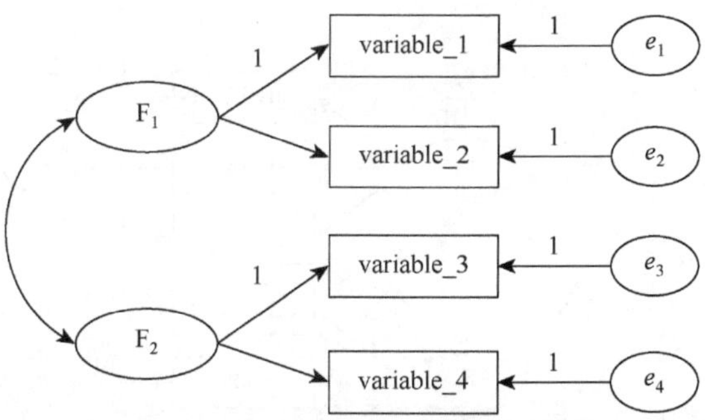

Figure 4.2 Different indicators having loadings on different common factors

In such models, one common factor has at least two indicators. For a model with both convergent validity and discrimination validity, factor loadings should be relatively high, while covariances (correlations) between different factors should be low.

C. The same indicator simultaneously having loadings on different factors

In a factor analysis model, an observed variable can simultaneously have loadings on different factors. The following is an example, in which variable_3 is assumed to have loadings on F_1 and F_2 simultaneously (Figure 4.3).

D. Second-order CFA models

The three types of CFA models discussed above can all be called first-order factor analysis models, in which the factors are estimated by observed variables. Such factors

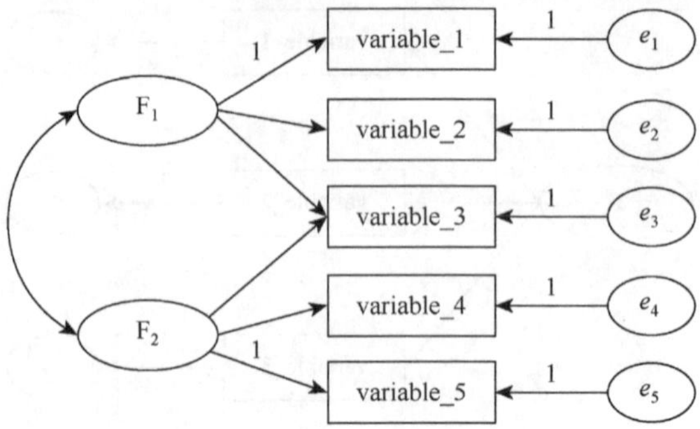

Figure 4.3 Indicators simultaneously having loadings on different factors

are first-order factors. Second-order CFA models are a kind of hierarchical factor analysis models, in which one or more factors are estimated by first-order factors rather than observed variables. For example, in the following model, factor F_3 is estimated by factor F_1 and factor F_2, which are related to their indicators. F_3 is a second-order factor, while F_1 and F_2 are first-order factors (Figure 4.4).

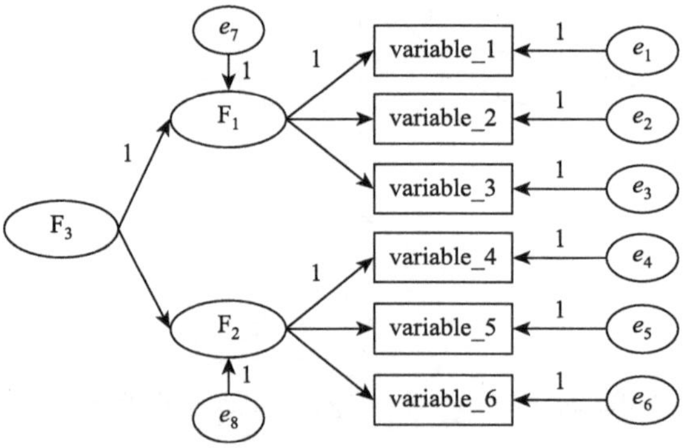

Figure 4.4 A second-order confirmative factor analysis model

4.1.1.2 Explorative factor analysis models

The factor analysis is called explorative factor analysis (EFA) if the purpose is to decide the number of factors needed to account for the relationships among a group of observed variables. Amos uses specification search for EFA. In a specification search, the relationships between the factors and the observed variables are all set to be optional, and the program is trusted to decide the relationships. For example, if we assume that two factors may explain the relationships among variable_1, variable_2, variable_3 and variable_4, we can draw the following model, in which the arrows from the factors to the observed variables are all optional (Figure 4.5). The specification search program will decide whether the two factors are capable of explaining the relationships, and which arrows are to be retained. In an EFA, the factor variance should be set at a fixed value to achieve model identification.

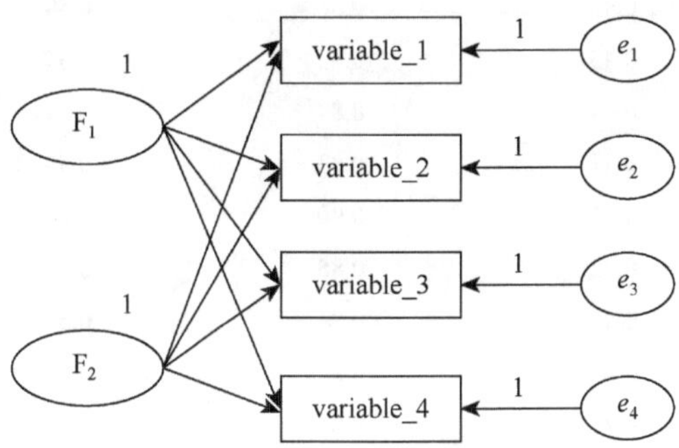

Figure 4.5 EFA model

4.1.2 Example of CFA with Different Indicators Having Loadings on Different Factors

Such models have two or more factors. As exogenous variables, the factors are correlated by default. To achieve model identification, each factor should have a regression weight set at a fixed value. Each observed variable has an error term. Now the application will be illustrated by the following example.

4.1.2.1 Dataset and task

The data were collected from a sample of 103 university students. The participants were required to produce speeches. The transcript of the speeches was further assessed in terms of 1) frequency of chunks (CHF), 2) variety of chunks (CHV), 3) ratio of error-free T-units (REFT), and 4) mean length of C-units after pruning (MLCP).

The data are presented in Table 4.1. In the data analysis, we want to test our assumption that a two-factor model can explain the four indexes: One factor is the chunk using skill (CHUS), which explains the CHF and CHV, and the other factor is speaking fluency (SF), which accounts for the REFT and the MLCP.

Table 4.1 Data for assessing students' speeches in English

Number	CHF	CHV	REFT	MLCP
1	0.43	0.81	0.56	7.70
2	0.47	0.85	0.56	9.70
3	0.43	0.81	0.55	7.70
4	0.46	0.87	0.62	7.70
5	0.46	0.86	0.59	6.70
6	0.43	0.82	0.57	8.70
7	0.44	0.84	0.59	11.70
8	0.41	0.83	0.59	10.70
9	0.47	0.90	0.62	14.70
10	0.43	0.85	0.58	7.70
11	0.41	0.84	0.57	9.70
12	0.45	0.85	0.59	10.70
13	0.45	0.84	0.61	9.70
14	0.43	0.86	0.55	8.70
15	0.42	0.82	0.59	12.70
16	0.45	0.86	0.58	9.70
17	0.42	0.82	0.58	7.70
18	0.41	0.79	0.60	10.70
19	0.46	0.86	0.58	10.70
20	0.49	0.87	0.58	10.70
21	0.45	0.85	0.58	8.70
22	0.48	0.85	0.60	15.70
23	0.49	0.90	0.57	7.70
24	0.43	0.85	0.60	12.70
25	0.49	0.89	0.59	12.70
26	0.43	0.86	0.57	7.70
27	0.43	0.82	0.59	11.70
28	0.42	0.82	0.54	5.70
29	0.43	0.84	0.62	15.70
30	0.42	0.83	0.50	2.70
31	0.43	0.84	0.60	9.70
32	0.45	0.83	0.58	7.70
33	0.43	0.83	0.57	10.70
34	0.43	0.82	0.58	7.70
35	0.47	0.85	0.57	8.70
36	0.44	0.85	0.51	9.70

Continued

Number	CHF	CHV	REFT	MLCP
37	0.43	0.84	0.60	15.70
38	0.47	0.87	0.58	7.70
39	0.43	0.83	0.58	9.70
40	0.46	0.85	0.62	15.70
41	0.44	0.83	0.57	8.70
42	0.45	0.84	0.55	5.70
43	0.45	0.85	0.56	7.70
44	0.46	0.85	0.59	11.70
45	0.44	0.84	0.56	8.70
46	0.46	0.84	0.60	10.70
47	0.47	0.89	0.61	13.70
48	0.44	0.82	0.57	5.70
49	0.44	0.83	0.56	9.70
50	0.50	0.88	0.61	11.70
51	0.48	0.87	0.63	15.70
52	0.42	0.83	0.57	7.70
53	0.42	0.80	0.56	9.70
54	0.39	0.81	0.55	7.70
55	0.46	0.86	0.55	6.70
56	0.52	0.90	0.61	12.70
57	0.46	0.88	0.59	10.70
58	0.43	0.84	0.58	10.70
59	0.42	0.82	0.58	8.70
60	0.45	0.87	0.62	11.70
61	0.46	0.87	0.60	13.70
62	0.46	0.83	0.54	7.70
63	0.44	0.85	0.60	14.70
64	0.45	0.86	0.60	9.70
65	0.40	0.81	0.57	6.70
66	0.46	0.87	0.56	5.70
67	0.45	0.86	0.64	13.70
68	0.41	0.81	0.53	0.70
69	0.51	0.88	0.60	9.70
70	0.43	0.84	0.53	4.70
71	0.47	0.84	0.57	9.70
72	0.41	0.81	0.56	8.70

Continued

Number	CHF	CHV	REFT	MLCP
73	0.42	0.82	0.54	7.70
74	0.42	0.81	0.54	3.70
75	0.44	0.84	0.59	9.70
76	0.41	0.87	0.61	7.70
77	0.45	0.89	0.56	5.70
78	0.42	0.81	0.60	14.70
79	0.38	0.78	0.55	3.70
80	0.49	0.87	0.59	7.70
81	0.43	0.85	0.57	7.70
82	0.44	0.85	0.60	5.70
83	0.44	0.86	0.63	14.70
84	0.43	0.86	0.58	6.70
85	0.44	0.86	0.56	7.70
86	0.44	0.83	0.58	7.70
87	0.42	0.83	0.59	11.70
88	0.42	0.82	0.60	11.70
89	0.41	0.82	0.56	3.70
90	0.48	0.83	0.53	3.70
91	0.43	0.84	0.54	5.70
92	0.45	0.85	0.57	8.70
93	0.43	0.84	0.57	11.70
94	0.41	0.84	0.63	13.70
95	0.44	0.83	0.56	8.70
96	0.40	0.84	0.57	6.70
97	0.43	0.83	0.60	11.70
98	0.43	0.84	0.58	7.70
99	0.44	0.84	0.57	6.70
100	0.41	0.83	0.56	5.70
101	0.43	0.82	0.60	11.70
102	0.40	0.82	0.56	4.70
103	0.42	0.87	0.58	10.70

The hypothesized relationships are shown in the following model (Figure 4.6).

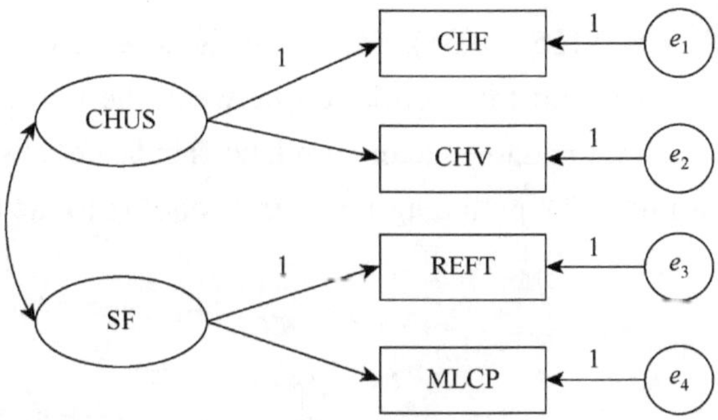

Figure 4.6 CFA model with different indicators having loadings on different common factors

4.1.2.2 Estimation results

Run the analysis, and we can get the results as follows (Table 4.2 and Table 4.3).

Table 4.2 Summary for a CFA model with different indicators having loadings on different common factors

Variables	Values
Number of distinct sample moments	10
Number of distinct parameters to be estimated	9
df	1
χ^2	2.231
p	0.135

Table 4.3 Selected estimation results for a CFA model with different indicators having loadings on different common factors

Variables	Estimates	S.E.	C.R.	*p*
Regression weights				
CHF<---CHUS	1.000			
CHV<---CHUS	1.229	0.287	4.286	***
REFT<---SF	1.000			
MLCP<---SF	96.893	20.941	4.627	***
Standardized regression weights				
CHF<---CHUS	0.746			
CHV<---CHUS	0.981			
REFT<---SF	0.962			
MLCP<---SF	0.776			
Correlation				
CHUS<-->SF	0.402			

With $\chi^2 = 2.231$ ($p = 0.135 > 0.05$), the model is acceptable. The factor loadings range from 0.746 to 0.981, and the correlation between the two factors is 0.402. The relatively high factor loadings and low factor correlations indicate satisfactory convergence and discrimination validity. The path diagram corresponding to the text output is like as follows (Figure 4.7).

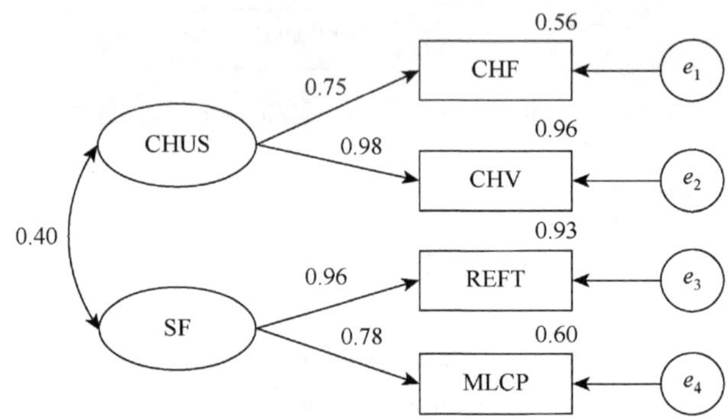

Figure 4.7 Standardized graphic output for a CFA model with different indicators having loadings on different common factors

4.1.2.3 Further confirmation of the acceptable model

To further confirm our model, we can repeat the analysis with competing models. For example, we can run the analysis with a model as shown in Figure 4.8.

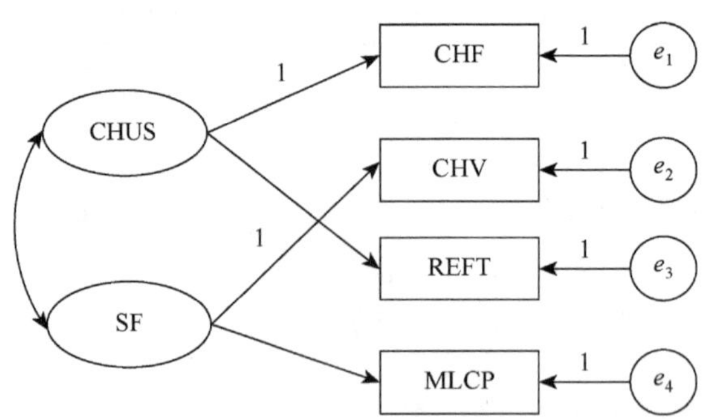

Figure 4.8 Competing model for confirming a concerned model

Run the analysis, and we will get the warning results as shown in Table 4.4.

Table 4.4 Warning covariance matrix for a competing model used for confirming a concerned model

Variables	SF	CHUS
SF	0.000	
CHUS	0.000	0.000

Note: The covariance matrix is not positive definite

"The following covariance matrix is not positive definite" is a warning message which suggests that the model is not correct. Providing evidence that the competing models are incorrect can further confirm the validity and acceptability of a concerned pre-existing model.

4.1.3 Example of CFA Involving Second-order Factors

Second-order CFA is similar to first-order CFA except that in such models the second-order factors are exogenous variables, while the first-order factors are endogenous variables, each of which has an error term. Moreover, indirect effects (the effects of the second-order factors on the observed variables) can be estimated in a second-order CFA. The application is illustrated with the example below.

4.1.3.1 Dataset and task

The data were collected through an oral interview and a questionnaire, including CHF, CHV, REFT, MLCP, fear of negative evaluation (FNE), communication apprehension (CA), trait anxiety (TA), and unwillingness to communicate (UTC). The last 4 variables were examined by rating scales (questionnaires). A total of 88 participants were involved in the in investigation. The data are displayed in Table 4.5.

Table 4.5 Data for a second-order factor analysis model

Number	CHF	CHV	REFT	MLCP	FNE	CA	TA	UTC
1	0.43	0.81	0.56	7.70	3.09	2.83	3.50	2.75
2	0.47	0.85	0.56	9.70	2.73	3.17	2.50	2.50
3	0.43	0.81	0.55	7.70	3.82	3.50	2.75	2.25
4	0.46	0.87	0.62	7.70	2.27	2.42	3.00	3.25
5	0.46	0.86	0.59	6.70	2.91	2.75	3.00	3.00
6	0.43	0.82	0.57	8.70	1.91	1.83	1.75	2.75
7	0.44	0.84	0.59	11.70	3.09	3.42	2.00	3.75

Continued

Number	CHF	CHV	REFT	MLCP	FNE	CA	TA	UTC
8	0.41	0.83	0.59	10.70	2.82	2.58	2.00	2.50
9	0.47	0.90	0.62	14.70	2.18	2.42	3.00	2.50
10	0.43	0.85	0.58	7.70	3.45	3.25	2.00	2.50
11	0.41	0.84	0.57	9.70	2.91	2.92	2.00	3.50
12	0.45	0.85	0.59	10.70	2.82	3.17	2.50	4.00
13	0.45	0.84	0.61	9.70	4.73	4.50	2.25	2.25
14	0.43	0.86	0.55	8.70	3.73	3.50	3.25	4.00
15	0.42	0.82	0.59	12.70	2.55	2.83	2.00	3.00
16	0.45	0.86	0.58	9.70	4.00	3.92	2.00	2.50
17	0.42	0.82	0.58	7.70	2.36	2.42	2.25	2.50
18	0.41	0.79	0.60	10.70	4.09	4.08	4.00	3.50
19	0.46	0.86	0.58	10.70	2.64	2.58	2.25	3.00
20	0.49	0.87	0.58	10.70	2.36	2.08	1.75	1.75
21	0.45	0.85	0.58	8.70	2.91	2.50	1.25	1.75
22	0.48	0.85	0.60	15.70	4.00	3.83	2.50	3.00
23	0.49	0.90	0.57	7.70	2.36	2.42	1.75	2.00
24	0.43	0.85	0.60	12.70	3.64	3.83	2.00	3.50
25	0.49	0.89	0.59	12.70	3.27	3.92	2.25	3.00
26	0.43	0.86	0.57	7.70	2.82	2.75	2.00	2.25
27	0.43	0.82	0.59	11.70	2.82	2.75	2.75	2.50
28	0.42	0.82	0.54	5.70	3.82	3.58	2.00	2.75
29	0.43	0.84	0.62	15.70	2.36	2.17	2.25	1.75
30	0.42	0.83	0.50	2.70	2.45	2.25	1.50	1.00
31	0.43	0.84	0.60	9.70	4.00	4.08	3.00	4.25
32	0.45	0.83	0.58	7.70	3.64	3.75	3.00	3.50
33	0.43	0.83	0.57	10.70	3.00	2.92	3.00	2.75
34	0.43	0.82	0.58	7.70	3.64	3.25	3.00	2.25
35	0.47	0.85	0.57	8.70	3.18	2.58	2.50	3.50
36	0.44	0.85	0.51	9.70	3.27	3.58	2.75	3.25
37	0.43	0.84	0.60	15.70	1.18	1.50	2.75	2.00
38	0.47	0.87	0.58	7.70	3.45	3.08	2.50	2.50
39	0.43	0.83	0.58	9.70	2.55	2.17	1.50	2.75
40	0.46	0.85	0.62	15.70	3.09	2.83	2.00	1.00
41	0.44	0.83	0.57	8.70	2.64	2.33	2.25	2.75
42	0.45	0.84	0.55	5.70	3.64	3.17	1.75	2.00
43	0.45	0.85	0.56	7.70	2.45	2.58	2.25	3.25

Continued

Number	CHF	CHV	REFT	MLCP	FNE	CA	TA	UTC
44	0.46	0.85	0.59	11.70	3.55	3.17	2.75	4.00
45	0.44	0.84	0.56	8.70	3.09	3.00	3.75	3.00
46	0.46	0.84	0.60	10.70	3.00	3.17	2.50	2.50
47	0.47	0.89	0.61	13.70	3.91	3.67	2.75	2.50
48	0.44	0.82	0.57	5.70	2.55	2.25	3.50	3.25
49	0.44	0.83	0.56	9.70	3.45	3.33	2.50	2.75
50	0.50	0.88	0.61	11.70	2.00	1.92	2.00	3.00
51	0.48	0.87	0.63	15.70	3.55	3.08	2.00	3.75
52	0.42	0.83	0.57	7.70	2.91	2.67	2.00	2.75
53	0.42	0.80	0.56	9.70	2.18	2.58	3.25	2.75
54	0.39	0.81	0.55	7.70	2.91	2.83	3.00	3.25
55	0.46	0.86	0.55	6.70	3.09	2.67	2.50	3.75
56	0.52	0.90	0.61	12.70	3.27	3.00	3.00	4.25
57	0.46	0.88	0.59	10.70	4.55	4.75	2.25	2.75
58	0.43	0.84	0.58	10.70	3.82	3.67	3.75	4.25
59	0.42	0.82	0.58	8.70	2.36	2.17	1.75	2.25
60	0.45	0.87	0.62	11.70	2.82	2.67	1.25	2.00
61	0.46	0.87	0.60	13.70	2.55	2.33	2.75	2.75
62	0.46	0.83	0.54	7.70	4.27	4.00	4.00	3.75
63	0.44	0.85	0.60	14.70	2.45	2.83	3.00	3.25
64	0.45	0.86	0.60	9.70	2.91	2.58	2.25	3.25
65	0.40	0.81	0.57	6.70	4.09	4.00	2.25	2.75
66	0.46	0.87	0.56	5.70	3.91	4.00	2.75	3.25
67	0.45	0.86	0.64	13.70	2.64	2.25	1.75	2.25
68	0.41	0.81	0.53	0.70	3.64	3.75	2.25	3.75
69	0.51	0.88	0.60	9.70	2.73	2.25	1.50	1.00
70	0.43	0.84	0.53	4.70	4.27	3.83	3.25	4.50
71	0.47	0.84	0.57	9.70	2.91	2.75	2.50	2.75
72	0.41	0.81	0.56	8.70	3.82	3.83	1.50	3.00
73	0.42	0.82	0.54	7.70	2.45	2.17	3.00	2.00
74	0.42	0.81	0.54	3.70	3.82	3.33	2.00	3.25
75	0.44	0.84	0.59	9.70	2.82	2.75	2.50	2.50
76	0.41	0.87	0.61	7.70	4.00	3.58	3.25	3.75
77	0.45	0.89	0.56	5.70	3.18	2.92	3.00	3.00
78	0.42	0.81	0.60	14.70	3.82	3.17	3.25	2.50
79	0.38	0.78	0.55	3.70	3.36	3.67	1.50	2.25

Continued

Number	CHF	CHV	REFT	MLCP	FNE	CA	TA	UTC
80	0.49	0.87	0.59	7.70	2.45	2.67	2.50	3.50
81	0.43	0.85	0.57	7.70	3.73	3.08	3.25	4.25
82	0.44	0.85	0.60	5.70	3.45	3.33	2.75	2.75
83	0.44	0.86	0.63	14.70	2.36	2.67	1.50	2.75
84	0.43	0.86	0.58	6.70	2.91	3.25	2.50	1.00
85	0.44	0.86	0.56	7.70	2.64	2.50	2.50	3.00
86	0.44	0.83	0.58	7.70	3.09	2.92	2.50	3.75
87	0.42	0.83	0.59	11.70	3.64	3.33	3.25	3.50
88	0.42	0.82	0.60	11.70	1.09	1.58	3.00	2.00

We will build a model to test our assumption that CHF and CHV are indicators of the latent variable of CHUS, REFT and MLCP are indicators of the latent variable FLUE (fluency in English), FNE and CA are indicators of FLCA (foreign language classroom anxiety), and TA and UTC are indicators of TRAIT (personal trait). Besides, CHUS and FLCA are influenced by a second-order factor LANG (language ability), while FLUE and TRAIT are influenced by another second-order factor PERS (personality). The model is like as follows (Figure 4.9).

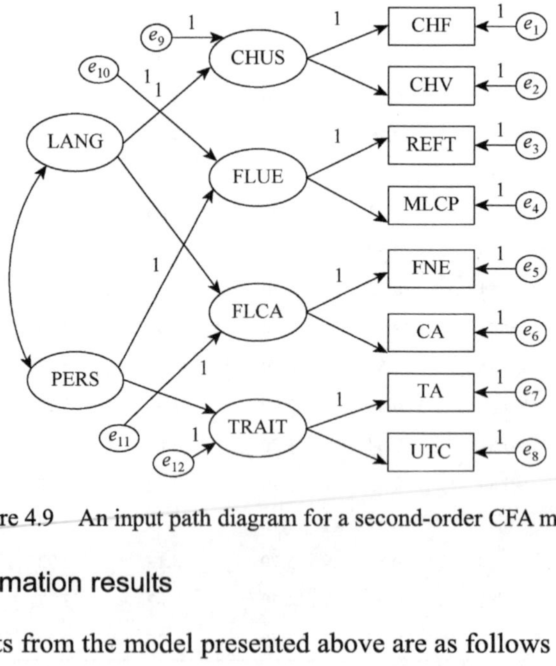

Figure 4.9 An input path diagram for a second-order CFA model

4.1.3.2 Estimation results

Selected results from the model presented above are as follows (Table 4.6).

Table 4.6 Warning covariance matrix for a second-order CFA model concerned

Variables	PERS	LANG
PERS	0.000	
LANG	0.000	0.000

Note: The covariance matrix is not positive definite

The information in Table 4.6 suggests that the solution is inadmissible. This implies that the model is not acceptable. To get an acceptable result, we can try competing models or trust Amos to decide the relationships with specification search. If specification search is used, the factor analysis is explorative in nature. In the next section, we will employ specification search to find a solution for the present problem.

4.1.4 Examples of EFA

EFA can be used when we do not have enough experience or knowledge to specify a model, or when the model we specified is not acceptable. To perform an EFA, we can turn to the specification search capacity of Amos. In a specification search, we have to set the variance (rather than the regression weight) of each factor at an arbitrary positive value to achieve model identification. Undecided relationships are all made optional and the program will decide which relationships are to be kept. Now we will use the dataset presented in Table 4.5 to perform a specification search to decide the relationships between the second-order factors and the first-order factors.

4.1.4.1 Modeling with Amos Graphics

Let's begin with a path diagram like Figure 4.9 (see Section 4.1.3.1). Replace the second-order factor names with "A" and "B" (or any other arbitrary labels). Draw single-headed arrows from A and B to each of the first-ordered factors. For the identification purpose, fix the variances of A and B at 1 (or any other positive values), and remove the constraints on any of the regression weights for predicting the first-order factors from A and B. From the menu, select "Analyze" and then "Specification Search" (Figure 4.10).

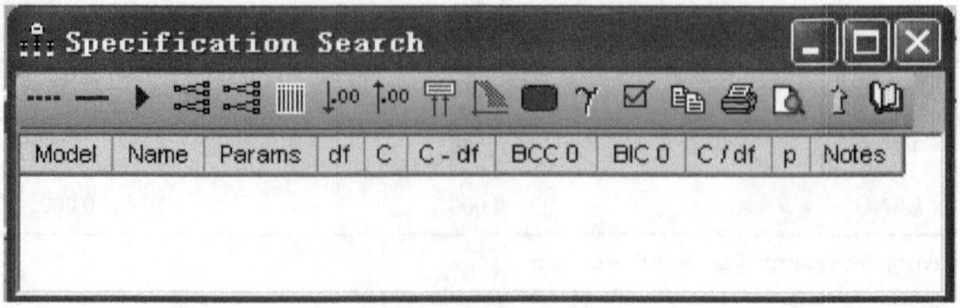

Figure 4.10 "Specification Search" window

Click the ---- menu in the "Specification Search" window, and click each of the arrows pointing from A and B to the first-order factors to make them optional. When this is completed, the model should look like as follows (Figure 4.11).

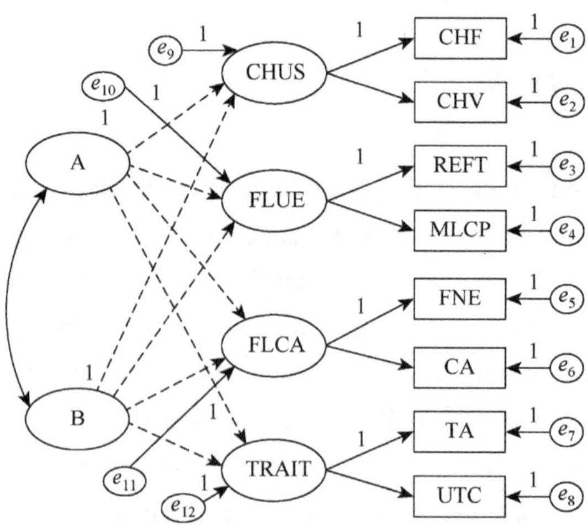

Figure 4.11 A model ready for specification search

4.1.4.2 Estimation results

When the setting shown above is finished, click ▶ in the "Specification Search" window to start the searching. When the searching process stops, click "p" at the top of the output summary table, and you can see two models with acceptable *p* values (Figure 4.12). Your searching results may not be exactly the same as what is displayed here due to the different settings.

Double-click the rows with acceptable *p* values, and we will find two models (Model A and Model B) in the Amos Graphics windows (Figure 4.13). CHUS and FLUE

Specification Search

Model	Name	Params	df	C	C - df	BCC 0	BIC 0	C / df	p	Notes
5	Default model	21	15	9.544	**-5.456**	**0.000**	**0.000**	**0.636**	**0.847**	
245	Default model	21	15	9.544	**-5.456**	**0.000**	**0.000**	**0.636**	**0.847**	
Sat	[Saturated]	36	0	0.000	0.000	23.917	57.616			
93	Default model	21	15	18.615	3.615	9.071	9.071	1.241	0.232	Inadmissible
171	Default model	21	15	18.615	3.615	9.071	9.071	1.241	0.232	Inadmissible
63	Default model	21	15	19.732	4.732	10.188	10.188	1.315	0.182	Inadmissible
201	Default model	21	15	19.732	4.732	10.188	10.188	1.315	0.182	Inadmissible

Figure 4.12 Summary of the specification results

are related to factor B in Model A, but to factor A in Model B. FLCA and TRAIT are related to factor A in model A, but to factor B in Model B. Model A and Model B are essentially the same, because the names of factors in Model A and Model B are simply arbitrarily selected labels.

In the model, CHUS and FLUE share a common factor, while FLCA and TRAIT share another common factor. The result is justifiable on theoretical grounds. CHUS and FLUE both belong to language competence. FLCA and TRAIT both subsume to personality.

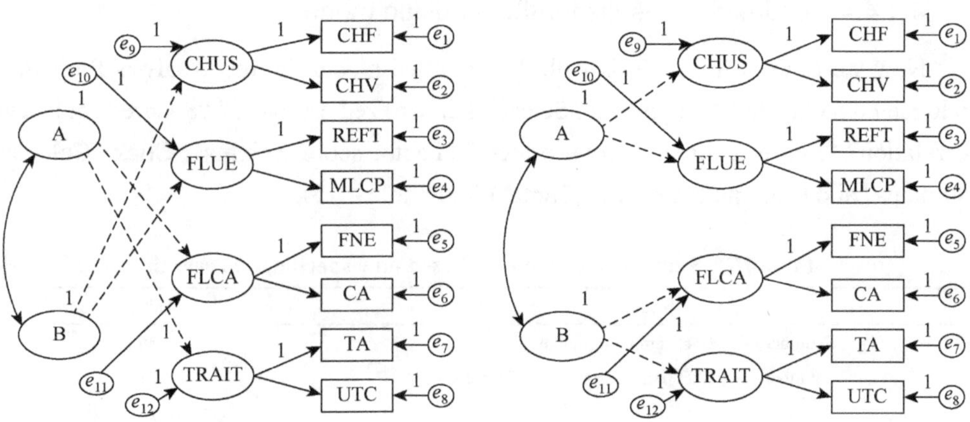

Figure 4.13 Graphic results from the specification search

4.1.4.3 Creating a model based on the specification search

Recall that in Section 4.1.3.1, we have a model represented by Figure 4.9. That model is unacceptable. With the outcome from the specification search, we can create a new model, which can be considered as a modification or substitute for the one represented by Figure 4.9. Based on the theoretical ground, in the new model we can name the label A as LANG and label B as PERS. Therefore, the factor labels A and B should be replaced by LANG and PERS. In the Amos Graphics window, the model should be modified as follows (Figure 4.14).

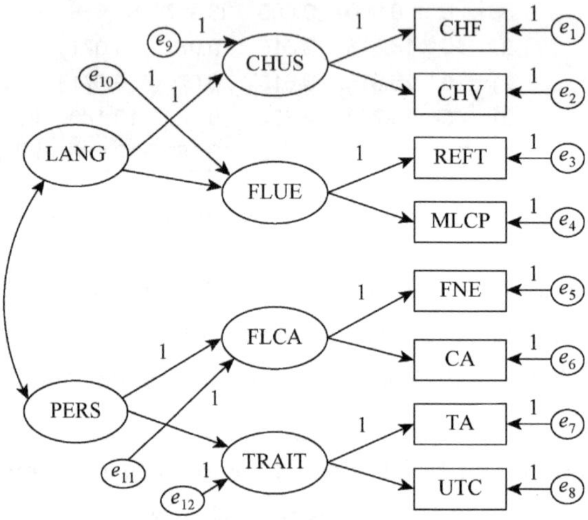

Figure 4.14 A modified model based on the specification search

4.1.4.4 Estimation results for the modified model

Now we can run the analysis with the modified model. In the "Analysis Properties" dialogue box, click the "Output" tab. Select "Standardized estimates" "Squared multilevel correlation" "Indirect, direct & total effects" "Factor score weights". Click "Calculate estimates" and examine the results (Table 4.7 to Table 4.15).

Table 4.7 Summary for a model based on a specification search

Variables	Values
Number of distinct sample moments	36
Number of distinct parameters to be estimated	21
df	15
χ^2	9.544
p	0.847

Table 4.8 Selected estimation results for a model based on a specification search

Variables	Estimates	S.E.	C.R.	*p*
Regression weights				
CHUS<---LANG	1.000			

Continued

Variables	Estimates	S.E.	C.R.	p
TRAIT<---PERS	0.261	0.329	0.793	0.428
FLCA<---PERS	1.000			
FLUE<---LANG	2.271	2.606	0.872	0.383
CHF<---CHUS	1.000			
CHV<---CHUS	1.086	0.212	5.111	***
REFT<---FLUE	1.000			
MLCP<---FLUE	98.022	20.900	4.690	***
FNE<---FLCA	1.000			
CA<---FLCA	0.948	0.104	9.140	***
TA<---TRAIT	1.000			
UTC<---TRAIT	2.049	0.865	2.370	0.018
Standardized regression weights				
CHUS<---LANG	0.475			
TRAIT<---PERS	0.479			
FLCA<---PERS	0.915			
FLUE<---LANG	0.939			
CHF<---CHUS	0.835			
CHV<---CHUS	0.928			
REFT<---FLUE	0.936			
MLCP<---FLUE	0.779			
FNE<---FLCA	0.956			
CA<---FLCA	0.958			
TA<---TRAIT	0.528			
UTC<---TRAIT	0.887			
Covariances				
LANG<-->PERS	−0.001	0.002	−0.801	0.423
Correlation				
LANG<-->PERS	−0.215			
Variances				
LANG	0.000	0.000	0.805	0.421
PERS	0.365	0.439	0.831	0.406
e_9	0.000	0.000	2.385	0.017
e_{10}	0.000	0.001	0.118	0.906
e_{12}	0.083	0.050	1.650	0.099
e_{11}	0.071	0.432	0.164	0.870

Continued

Variables	Estimates	S.E.	C.R.	*p*
e_1	0.000	0.000	2.267	0.023
e_2	0.000	0.000	0.887	0.375
e_3	0.000	0.000	0.721	0.471
e_4	3.764	1.263	2.981	0.003
e_6	0.035	0.039	0.883	0.377
e_8	0.122	0.178	0.685	0.493
e_5	0.041	0.044	0.931	0.352
e_7	0.279	0.060	4.668	***
Squared multiple correlations				
TRAIT	0.230			
FLCA	0.837			
FLUE	0.882			
CHUS	0.225			
UTC	0.788			
TA	0.279			
CA	0.918			
FNE	0.914			
MLCP	0.607			
REFT	0.877			
CHV	0.861			
CHF	0.698			

Table 4.9 Factor score weights for a model based on a specification search

Variables	UTC	TA	CA	FNE	MLCP	REFT	CHV	CHF
PERS	0.073	0.016	0.412	0.370	–0.002	–0.683	–0.085	–0.034
LANG	0.000	0.000	0.000	0.000	0.001	0.270	0.033	0.013
TRAIT	0.340	0.073	0.026	0.023	0.000	–0.043	–0.005	–0.002
FLCA	0.016	0.003	0.513	0.461	0.000	–0.150	–0.019	–0.007
FLUE	0.000	0.000	0.000	0.000	0.002	0.718	0.038	0.015
CHUS	0.000	0.000	0.000	0.000	0.000	0.035	0.588	0.237

Table 4.10 Total effects for a model based on a specification search

Variables	PERS	LANG	TRAIT	FLCA	FLUE	CHUS
TRAIT	0.261	0.000	0.000	0.000	0.000	0.000
FLCA	1.000	0.000	0.000	0.000	0.000	0.000

Continued

Variables	PERS	LANG	TRAIT	FLCA	FLUE	CHUS
FLUE	0.000	2.271	0.000	0.000	0.000	0.000
CHUS	0.000	1.000	0.000	0.000	0.000	0.000
UTC	0.534	0.000	2.049	0.000	0.000	0.000
TA	0.261	0.000	1.000	0.000	0.000	0.000
CA	0.948	0.000	0.000	0.948	0.000	0.000
FNE	1.000	0.000	0.000	1.000	0.000	0.000
MLCP	0.000	222.630	0.000	0.000	98.022	0.000
REFT	0.000	2.271	0.000	0.000	1.000	0.000
CHV	0.000	1.086	0.000	0.000	0.000	1.086
CHF	0.000	1.000	0.000	0.000	0.000	1.000

Table 4.11 Standardized total effects for a model based on a specification search

Variables	PERS	LANG	TRAIT	FLCA	FLUE	CHUS
TRAIT	0.479	0.000	0.000	0.000	0.000	0.000
FLCA	0.915	0.000	0.000	0.000	0.000	0.000
FLUE	0.000	0.939	0.000	0.000	0.000	0.000
CHUS	0.000	0.475	0.000	0.000	0.000	0.000
UTC	0.426	0.000	0.887	0.000	0.000	0.000
TA	0.253	0.000	0.528	0.000	0.000	0.000
CA	0.877	0.000	0.000	0.958	0.000	0.000
FNE	0.875	0.000	0.000	0.956	0.000	0.000
MLCP	0.000	0.732	0.000	0.000	0.779	0.000
REFT	0.000	0.879	0.000	0.000	0.936	0.000
CHV	0.000	0.441	0.000	0.000	0.000	0.928
CHF	0.000	0.396	0.000	0.000	0.000	0.835

Table 4.12 Direct effects for a model based on a specification search

Variables	PERS	LANG	TRAIT	FLCA	FLUE	CHUS
TRAIT	0.261	0.000	0.000	0.000	0.000	0.000
FLCA	1.000	0.000	0.000	0.000	0.000	0.000
FLUE	0.000	2.271	0.000	0.000	0.000	0.000
CHUS	0.000	1.000	0.000	0.000	0.000	0.000
UTC	0.000	0.000	2.049	0.000	0.000	0.000

Continued

Variables	PERS	LANG	TRAIT	FLCA	FLUE	CHUS
TA	0.000	0.000	1.000	0.000	0.000	0.000
CA	0.000	0.000	0.000	0.948	0.000	0.000
FNE	0.000	0.000	0.000	1.000	0.000	0.000
MLCP	0.000	0.000	0.000	0.000	98.022	0.000
REFT	0.000	0.000	0.000	0.000	1.000	0.000
CHV	0.000	0.000	0.000	0.000	0.000	1.086
CHF	0.000	0.000	0.000	0.000	0.000	1.000

Table 4.13 Standardized direct effects for a model based on a specification search

Variables	PERS	LANG	TRAIT	FLCA	FLUE	CHUS
TRAIT	0.479	0.000	0.000	0.000	0.000	0.000
FLCA	0.915	0.000	0.000	0.000	0.000	0.000
FLUE	0.000	0.939	0.000	0.000	0.000	0.000
CHUS	0.000	0.475	0.000	0.000	0.000	0.000
UTC	0.000	0.000	0.887	0.000	0.000	0.000
TA	0.000	0.000	0.528	0.000	0.000	0.000
CA	0.000	0.000	0.000	0.958	0.000	0.000
FNE	0.000	0.000	0.000	0.956	0.000	0.000
MLCP	0.000	0.000	0.000	0.000	0.779	0.000
REFT	0.000	0.000	0.000	0.000	0.936	0.000
CHV	0.000	0.000	0.000	0.000	0.000	0.928
CHF	0.000	0.000	0.000	0.000	0.000	0.835

Table 4.14 Indirect effects for a model based on a specification search

Variables	PERS	LANG	TRAIT	FLCA	FLUE	CHUS
TRAIT	0.000	0.000	0.000	0.000	0.000	0.000
FLCA	0.000	0.000	0.000	0.000	0.000	0.000
FLUE	0.000	0.000	0.000	0.000	0.000	0.000
CHUS	0.000	0.000	0.000	0.000	0.000	0.000
UTC	0.534	0.000	0.000	0.000	0.000	0.000
TA	0.261	0.000	0.000	0.000	0.000	0.000
CA	0.948	0.000	0.000	0.000	0.000	0.000
FNE	1.000	0.000	0.000	0.000	0.000	0.000

Continued

Variables	PERS	LANG	TRAIT	FLCA	FLUE	CHUS
MLCP	0.000	222.630	0.000	0.000	0.000	0.000
REFT	0.000	2.271	0.000	0.000	0.000	0.000
CHV	0.000	1.086	0.000	0.000	0.000	0.000
CHF	0.000	1.000	0.000	0.000	0.000	0.000

Table 4.15 Standardized indirect effects for a model based on a specification search

Variables	PERS	LANG	TRAIT	FLCA	FLUE	CHUS
TRAIT	0.000	0.000	0.000	0.000	0.000	0.000
FLCA	0.000	0.000	0.000	0.000	0.000	0.000
FLUE	0.000	0.000	0.000	0.000	0.000	0.000
CHUS	0.000	0.000	0.000	0.000	0.000	0.000
UTC	0.426	0.000	0.000	0.000	0.000	0.000
TA	0.253	0.000	0.000	0.000	0.000	0.000
CA	0.877	0.000	0.000	0.000	0.000	0.000
FNE	0.875	0.000	0.000	0.000	0.000	0.000
MLCP	0.000	0.732	0.000	0.000	0.000	0.000
REFT	0.000	0.879	0.000	0.000	0.000	0.000
CHV	0.000	0.441	0.000	0.000	0.000	0.000
CHF	0.000	0.396	0.000	0.000	0.000	0.000

In the table of factor score weights (Table 4.9), you can see the regression weights of unobserved variables on different observed variables. This table is displayed if factor score weights are selected in the "Analysis Properties" dialogue box.

Total effects, direct effects and indirect effects (Table 4.10-Table 4.15) are displayed if "Indirect, direct & total effects" is selected in the "Analysis Properties" dialogue box. Table 4.10 indicates the total effects (direct effects integrated with the indirect ones) of the column variables on the row variables. For example, a 1-point increase in PERS predicts a 0.261-point increase in TRAIT. Direct effects exist between variables directly connected by single-headed arrows. Indirect effects are the effects of one variable on another via one or more mediators. For example, PERS has an indirect effect on TA, as well as on UTC, via the mediator of TRAIT.

An indirect effect equals the product of all the direct effects existing between the two variables concerned. For example, the direct effect of PERS on TRAIT is 0.261, and that of TRAIT on TA is 1; therefore, the indirect effect of PERS on TA is $0.261 \times 1 = 0.261$. Standardized effects are unstandardized effects divided by the standard deviation. The standard path diagram output for the present model is as follows (Figure 4.15).

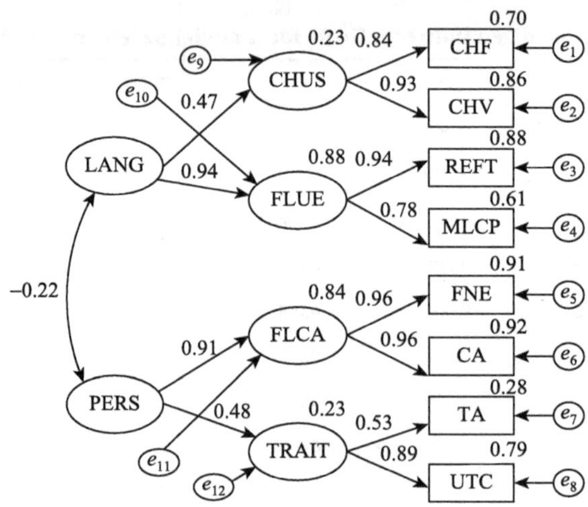

Figure 4.15 Graphic output for the model concerned

4.2 Structural Regression Models

In a factor analysis model, the researcher is primarily concerned with the relationships between observed variables and the corresponding factors. If the second-order factors are involved, the relationships between the second-order factors and the first-order factors are additional concerns. When two or more exogenous factors are involved in a model, correlations between the factors are also analyzed by default. There is, however, no regression existing between parallel factors. If we want to examine the regression of one factor on another parallel factor, we have to use a structural regression model. A structural regression model is similar to a path analysis model except that factors are used as model-building units. Figure 4.16 illustrates the differences among a simple factor analysis model, a structural regression model and a path analysis model.

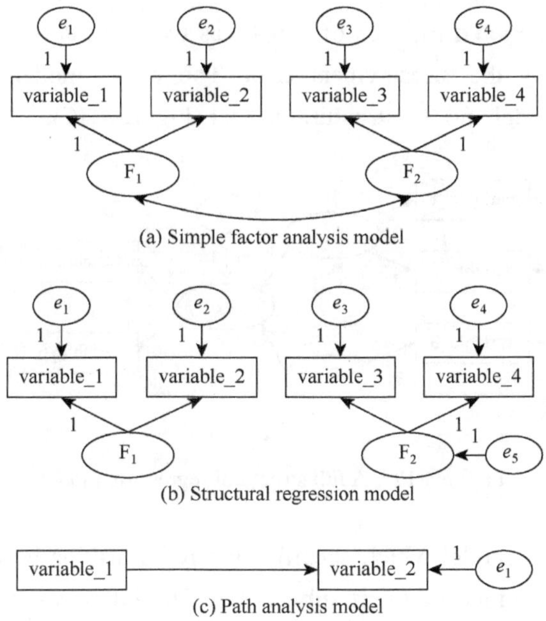

Figure 4.16 Comparison among simple factor analysis model, structural regression model and path analysis model

In a structural regression model, factors are also called latent variables. One latent variable is usually represented by two or more indicators. The estimated regression weight of an indicator on the latent variable is called measurement weight or factor loading.

4.2.1 Types of Elementary Structural Regression Models

Structural regression models can be classified in different ways. We can follow the way in which path models are classified, because every path model can be developed into a structural regression model if one or more of the observed variables are replaced by latent variables with indicators. But this classification method is not the characteristic of structural regression models. Here we will classify elementary structural regression models as full and partial structural regression models.

4.2.1.1 Full structural regression models

Full structural regression models are composed of measurement sub-models and structural sub-models. Let's take the following model for example. It has three latent variables, namely F_1, F_2 and F_3, each of which has two indicators. Each indicator has an error term, suggesting the measurement error. The whole model is composed of the measurement sub-model and the structural model (Figure 4.17).

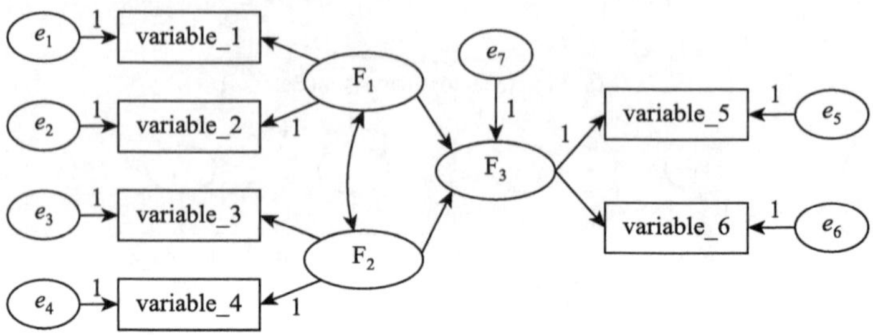

Figure 4.17 A full structural regression model

The portion of a model which specifies the relationships between indicators and latent variables is the measurement sub-model. One latent variable has at least two indicators (Figure 4.18).

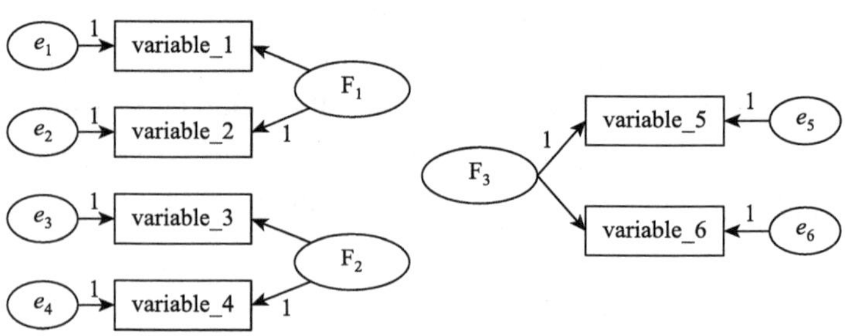

Figure 4.18 A measurement sub-model

The portion of a model which specifies how latent variables are related to each other is called the structural sub-model. The following diagram displays the structural sub-model, which suggests that the latent variable F_3 regresses on the latent variables F_1 and F_2 (Figure 4.19).

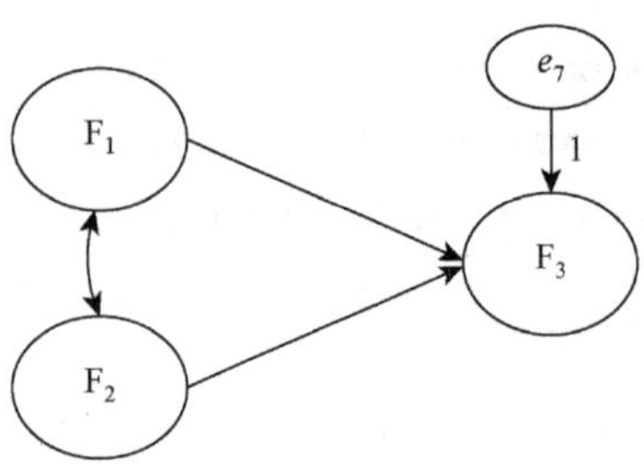

Figure 4.19 A structural sub-model

As in path analysis, latent variables should have an error term when used as endogenous variables. In the present example, F_3 is an endogenous latent variable and e_7 is its error term.

4.2.1.2 Partial structural regression models

A partial structural regression model is similar to a full structural regression model except that one or more latent variables in the structural sub-model are replaced by observed variables. For example, the following path diagram represents a partial structural regression model, in which variable_3 is an observed variable taking the place of a latent variable in the structural sub-model (Figure 4.20).

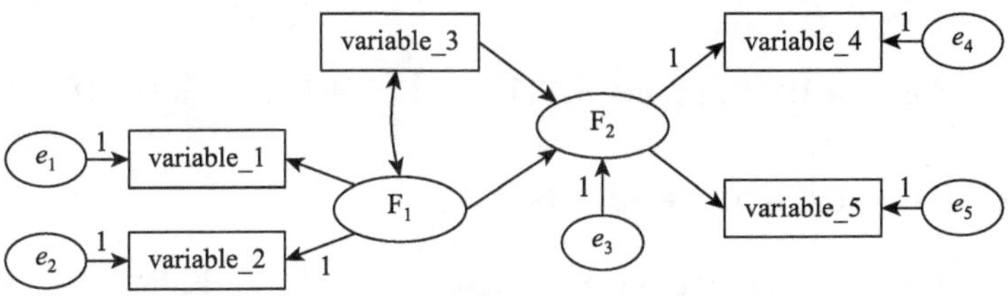

Figure 4.20 A partial structural regression model

In fact, partial structural regression models are combinations of structural regression and path models. Due to the involvement of an observed variable used as a predictor of a latent variable, the analysis of partial structural regression models differs from that of full structural regression models.

4.2.2 Examples of Full Structural Regression Analysis

In a full structural regression analysis, exogenous latent variables are correlated by default. Each of the endogenous variables has an error term. To achieve model identification, every latent variable must have a regression weight (or the variance) fixed at a specific value. The application is illustrated in the following example.

4.2.2.1 Data and task

In this example, we will make use of the dataset presented in Table 4.5. FLCA, CHUS, FLUE and TRAIT are considered as latent variables. CHF, CHV, REFT, MLCP, TA and UTC are the corresponding indicators. The regression of FLCA on CHUS, FLUE and TRAIT is to be analyzed. The path diagram for this analysis is as follows (Figure 4.21).

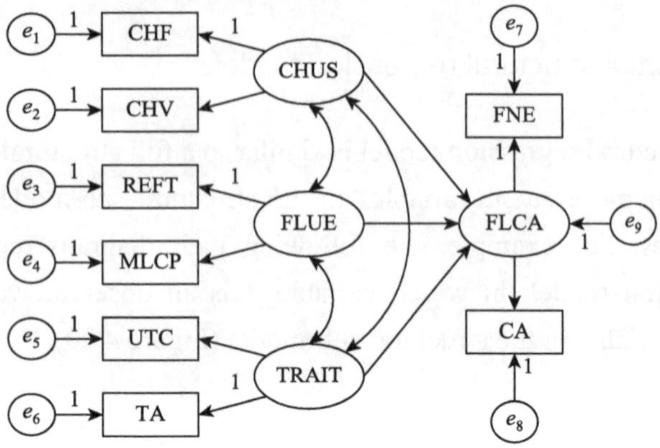

Figure 4.21 Regression of FLCA on CHUS, FLUE and TRAIT

4.2.2.2 Modeling and the results

To accomplish the task, we have to draw a model like Figure 4.21 in the Amos Graphics window. In the "Analysis Properties" dialogue box, keep "Standardized estimates" "Indirect, direct & total effects" "Factor score weights" selected. The text results for the model are displayed in Table 4.16 to Table 4.21.

Table 4.16 Summary for a full structural regression analysis

Variables	Values
Number of distinct sample moments	36
Number of distinct parameters to be estimated	22
df	14
χ^2	9.421
p	0.803

Table 4.17 Selected estimation results for a full structural regression analysis

Variables	Estimates	S.E.	C.R.	*p*
Regression weights				
FLCA<---CHUS	−1.088	3.755	−0.290	0.772
FLCA<---TRAIT	0.858	0.284	3.016	0.003
FLCA<---FLUE	−3.377	3.358	−1.006	0.315
TA<---TRAIT	1.000			
UTC<---TRAIT	2.148	0.938	2.289	0.022
CHF<---CHUS	1.000			
CHV<---CHUS	1.090	0.213	5.125	***

Continued

Variables	Estimates	S.E.	C.R.	p
MLCP<---FLUE	97.480	20.846	4.676	***
REFT<---FLUE	1.000			
CA<---FLCA	0.951	0.104	9.143	***
FNE<---FLCA	1.000			
Variances				
TRAIT	0.103	0.058	1.787	0.074
CHUS	0.000	0.000	3.646	***
FLUE	0.001	0.000	3.869	***
e_9	0.345	0.074	4.673	***
e_5	0.100	0.193	0.521	0.602
e_1	0.000	0.000	2.301	0.021
e_4	3.796	1.262	3.008	0.003
e_3	0.000	0.000	0.687	0.492
e_6	0.284	0.060	4.743	***
e_8	0.034	0.040	0.852	0.394
e_7	0.042	0.044	0.962	0.336
e_2	0.000	0.000	0.865	0.387
Squared multiple correlations				
FLCA	0.206			
FNE	0.912			
CA	0.921			
REFT	0.882			
MLCP	0.604			
CHV	0.865			
CHF	0.695			
UTC	0.826			
TA	0.266			

Table 4.18 Factor score weights for a full structural factor analysis

Variables	FNE	CA	REFT	MLCP	CHV	CHF	UTC	TA
FLUE	0.000	0.000	0.729	0.002	0.037	0.014	0.000	0.000
CHUS	0.000	0.000	0.035	0.000	0.593	0.230	0.000	0.000
TRAIT	0.018	0.021	−0.076	0.000	0.076	0.030	0.349	0.057
FLCA	0.445	0.529	−0.139	0.000	−0.038	−0.015	0.016	0.003

Table 4.19 Total effects for a full structural factor analysis

Variables	FLUE	CHUS	TRAIT	FLCA
FLCA	–3.377	–1.088	0.858	0.000
FNE	–3.377	–1.088	0.858	1.000
CA	–3.211	–1.034	0.816	0.951
REFT	1.000	0.000	0.000	0.000
MLCP	97.480	0.000	0.000	0.000
CHV	0.000	1.090	0.000	0.000
CHF	0.000	1.000	0.000	0.000
UTC	0.000	0.000	2.148	0.000
TA	0.000	0.000	1.000	0.000

Table 4.20 Direct effects for a full structural factor analysis

Variables	FLUE	CHUS	TRAIT	FLCA
FLCA	–3.377	–1.088	0.858	0.000
FNE	0.000	0.000	0.000	1.000
CA	0.000	0.000	0.000	0.951
REFT	1.000	0.000	0.000	0.000
MLCP	97.480	0.000	0.000	0.000
CHV	0.000	1.090	0.000	0.000
CHF	0.000	1.000	0.000	0.000
UTC	0.000	0.000	2.148	0.000
TA	0.000	0.000	1.000	0.000

Table 4.21 Indirect effects for a full structural factor analysis

Variables	FLUE	CHUS	TRAIT	FLCA
FLCA	0.000	0.000	0.000	0.000
FNE	–3.377	–1.088	0.858	0.000
CA	–3.211	–1.034	0.816	0.000
REFT	0.000	0.000	0.000	0.000
MLCP	0.000	0.000	0.000	0.000
CHV	0.000	0.000	0.000	0.000
CHF	0.000	0.000	0.000	0.000
UTC	0.000	0.000	0.000	0.000
TA	0.000	0.000	0.000	0.000

With $p>0.05$, the model is acceptable. The estimates indicate that all the regression weights are significant except that of FLCA on CHUS and FLUE. Variances for all the exogenous latent variables and error terms are estimated. The squared multiple correlation for FLCA (0.206) suggests that 20.6% of the variance of FLCA can be explained by all the predictors in the model. The squared multiple correlation for each indicator is a conservative estimate of the reliability. For example, the reliability for CA is at least 0.921, and for FNE is at least 0.912.

Table 4.18 displays the regression weights of each factor on all the observed variables in the model. For example, a 1-point increase in CHF predicts a 0.030-point increase in TRAIT.

Table 4.19 displays the total effect (the combination of direct effect and indirect effect) of each factor on each endogenous variable. For example, the total effect of TRAIT on FLCA is 0.858, which means that a 1-point increase on TRAIT predicts a 0.858-point increase on FLCA. The standardized path diagram output for the model is like as follows (Figure 4.22).

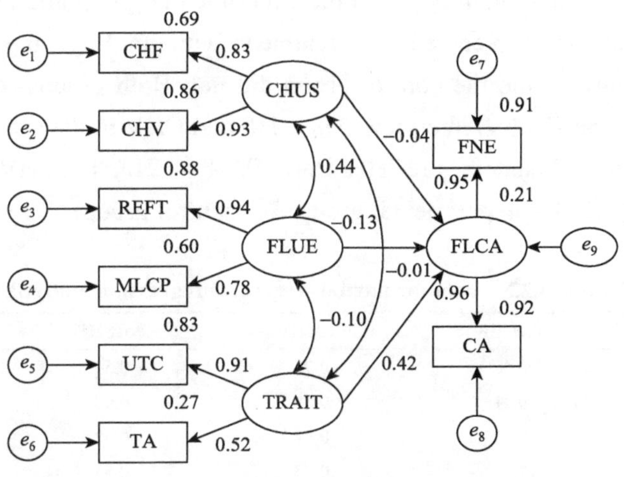

Figure 4.22 Graphic output of the full structural regression model

4.2.3 Examples of Partial Structural Regression Analysis

Covariance indicates the degree to which two variables change together. The analysis of covariance combines with the analysis of variance with regression. The purpose is to examine the effect of a categorically independent variable on the mean of a dependent variable while controlling the effects of other continuous variables (covariates). Pre-existing group differences related to the covariates are thus controlled.

Partial structural regression analysis can be employed for the analysis of covariance. In a partial structural regression model, the categorically independent variables and covariates are used as parallel predictors for the dependent variables. The categorically independent variable is an observed variable, while the covariates are latent variables. The measurement errors of the covariates can thus be estimated.

Employing a partial structural regression model has a great advantage over conventional techniques for the analysis of covariance. When conventional techniques are used, measurement errors of the covariates can lead to incorrect conclusions. But in a partial structural regression model, measurement errors are not a problem because they can be estimated and controlled in the analysis. The application is illustrated in the following section.

4.2.3.1 Dataset and task

Here is an example, in which 32 university students were involved in an experiment. They were randomly put in the experimental group and the control group. The experimental group received the treatment with an English speaking anxiety reduction procedure, while the control group did not. Both groups received a pretest and a posttest of oral English interview. The CHF and CHV in the speech in the pretest and posttest were calculated (PreCHF, PreCHV, PosCHF, PosCHV). The data are shown in Table 4.22 (1 = experimental group; 2 = control group).

Table 4.22 Data for partial structural regression analysis

Groups	PreCHF	PreCHV	PosCHF	PosCHV
1	0.42	0.73	0.51	0.72
1	0.41	0.75	0.48	0.82
1	0.42	0.81	0.52	0.82
1	0.51	0.75	0.57	0.82
1	0.42	0.75	0.50	0.81
1	0.51	0.83	0.60	0.90
1	0.51	0.93	0.60	0.93
1	0.48	0.91	0.58	0.97
1	0.45	0.84	0.53	0.83
1	0.42	0.81	0.51	0.84
1	0.47	0.81	0.58	0.91
1	0.43	0.73	0.53	0.83
1	0.51	0.93	0.61	0.98
1	0.45	0.78	0.50	0.81

Continued

Groups	PreCHF	PreCHV	PosCHF	PosCHV
1	0.46	0.79	0.53	0.85
2	0.37	0.76	0.47	0.83
2	0.47	0.84	0.43	0.76
2	0.36	0.71	0.40	0.73
2	0.50	0.87	0.63	0.80
2	0.33	0.65	0.41	0.71
2	0.50	0.89	0.47	0.81
2	0.37	0.76	0.38	0.73
2	0.52	0.91	0.42	0.81
2	0.52	0.83	0.62	0.91
2	0.52	0.87	0.38	0.74
2	0.33	0.71	0.42	0.78
2	0.41	0.72	0.45	0.79
2	0.33	0.69	0.37	0.72
2	0.42	0.82	0.52	0.86
2	0.47	0.83	0.58	0.89
2	0.37	0.74	0.36	0.72
2	0.52	0.92	0.61	0.97

Here PreCHF and PreCHV can be considered as indicators of the factor PreCHUS (the tendency to use chunks in the speech prior to the anxiety reduction treatment), while PosCHF and PosCHV as indicators of the factor PosCHUS (the tendency to use chunks in the speech succeeding the treatment). In this analysis, we will examine whether the treatment has a significant effect on PosCHUS.

4.2.3.2 Modeling with Amos Graphics

The effect of treatment can be revealed by the group effect. To control PreCHUS, we have to consider it as a covariate and examine group effect while controlling this covariate. To assess the group effect, we will perform the analysis in two stages. In the first stage, we will build an acceptable model and examine whether the regression of PosCHUS on the variable of group is significant; in the second stage, we will further examine whether the model is acceptable if the regression of PosCHUS on the variable of group is fixed at 0. Each stage will focus on a question. The question for the first stage can be expressed as follows: Is the regression of PosCHUS on group significant? We can create a path diagram like Figure 4.23 to help us answer the question. This is a partial structural regression model.

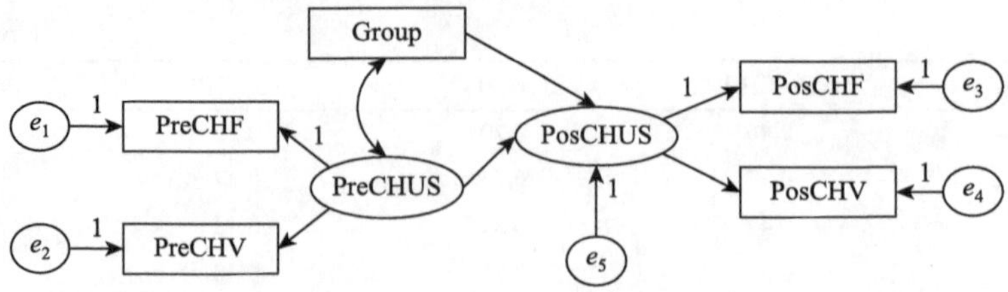

Figure 4.23 The regression of PosCHUS on group and PreCHUS

In this model, the group effect is separated from the PreCHUS. In other words, the PreCHUS is considered as a covariate and the effect is controlled.

4.2.3.3 Estimation results

Run the analysis for the model created above, and then we can obtain the text output. Table 4.23 is a summary of the model.

Table 4.23 Summary of the analysis of the partial structural regression model

Variables	Values
Number of distinct sample moments	15
Number of distinct parameters to be estimated	12
df	3
χ^2	11.110
p	0.011

With $\chi^2 = 11.110$, and $p = 0.011 < 0.05$, the model is not acceptable. To find clues for the modification of the model, we can examine the M.I. To request Amos to provide the M.I., we have to 1) open the "Analysis Properties" dialogue box; 2) click the "Output" tab, and select "Modification indices"; 3) close the "Analysis Properties" dialogue box and repeat the analysis. Click "Modification indices" in the navigation tree of the output window, and we can see the following results (Table 4.24).

Table 4.24 M.I. for the partial structural regression model

Covariances	M.I.	Par change
e_4 <--> e_2	5.911	0.001
e_4 <--> e_1	4.891	0.000
e_3 <--> e_2	5.762	−0.001
e_3 <--> e_1	4.660	0.001

The first column lists the parameters that could be freely estimated. Each M.I. value gives a conservative estimate of the χ^2 change if we repeat the analysis with the corresponding parameter freely estimated. The par change indicates the approximate parameter change in the new analysis.

4.2.3.4 Modifying the partial regression model

We should try to modify the setting of a single parameter and repeat the analysis each time. The setting of the parameter with a relatively large M.I. should be modified in the first trial if the modification is justifiable on theoretical grounds. In the present example, freely estimating the covariance between e_2 and e_4 may produce a relatively large M.I. (at least 5.911), and it is theoretically justifiable. The e_2 and e_4 are error terms related to the same kind of tests. It is plausible to assume that some common unknown factors may influence both the pretest and the posttest of the same type of skill (CHV). The improved model with the covariance between e_2 and e_4 freely estimated is like as follows (Figure 4.24).

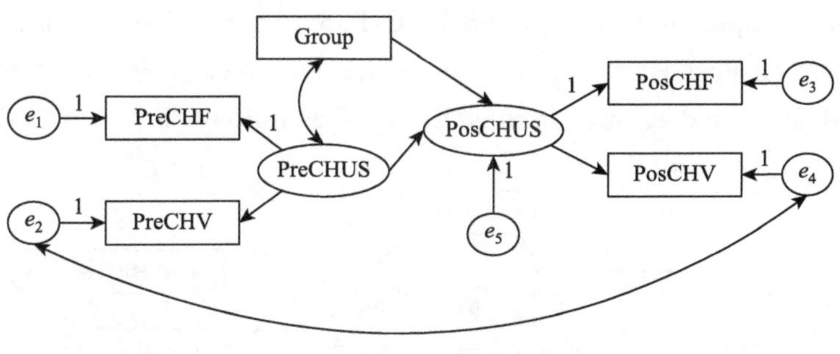

Figure 4.24 Regression of PosCHUS on group and PreCHUS: A modified model

4.2.3.5 Estimation results for the modified partial regression model

Now we can repeat the analysis with the model shown in Figure 4.24. Results are as follows (Table 4.25 and Table 4.26).

Table 4.25 Summary for a modified partial structural regression model

Variables	Values
Number of distinct sample moments	15
Number of distinct parameters to be estimated	13
df	2

Continued

Variables	Values
χ^2	1.115
p	0.573

Table 4.26 Regression weights for a modified partial structural regression model

Variables	Estimates	S.E.	C.R.	p
PosCHUS <--- Group	−0.055	0.019	−2.870	0.004
PosCHUS <--- PreCHUS	0.813	0.194	4.191	***
PosCHF <--- PosCHUS	1.000			
PosCHV <--- PosCHUS	0.890	0.126	7.047	***
PreCHF <--- PreCHUS	1.000			
PreCHV <--- PreCHUS	1.074	0.186	5.782	***

With $\chi^2 = 1.115$, $p = 0.573$, the model is acceptable. In this improved model, the regression weight of PosCHUS on group is significant ($\beta = -0.055$, $p = 0.004$) while the regression weight of PosCHUS on PreCHUS is controlled. In other words, the effect of group on PosCHUS is significant while the effect of PreCHUS is controlled. The standardized path diagram output is displayed as follows (Figure 4.25).

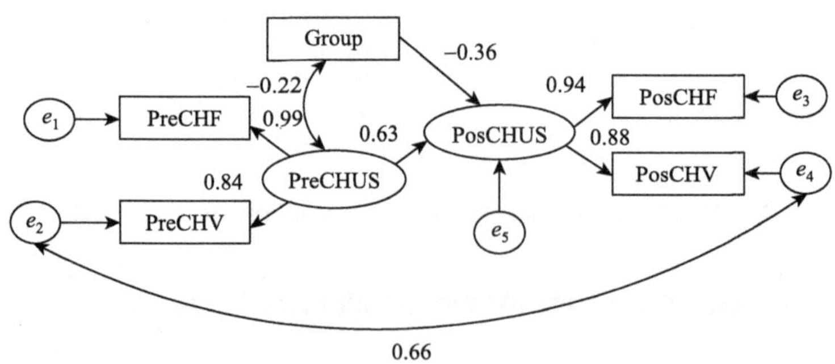

Figure 4.25 Graphic output for the modified partial regression model

4.2.3.6 Further modifying the acceptable model for confirmation of the results

Now we should continue with the second stage of the analysis. The question for this stage can be expressed as follows: Is the model acceptable when the regression of PosCHUS on group is fixed at 0? In the first stage, we have revealed a significant group effect. To confirm the result, we can change the model specification, set the regression weight of PosCHUS on group at 0, and repeat the analysis. This is a stronger test. Our finding in the first stage is supported if such a model is unacceptable. To change the setting, right-click the arrow from "Group" to "PosCHUS" and open the "Objcct Properties" dialogue box and select the "Parameters" tab and type "0" in the "Regression weight" text box (Figure 4.26).

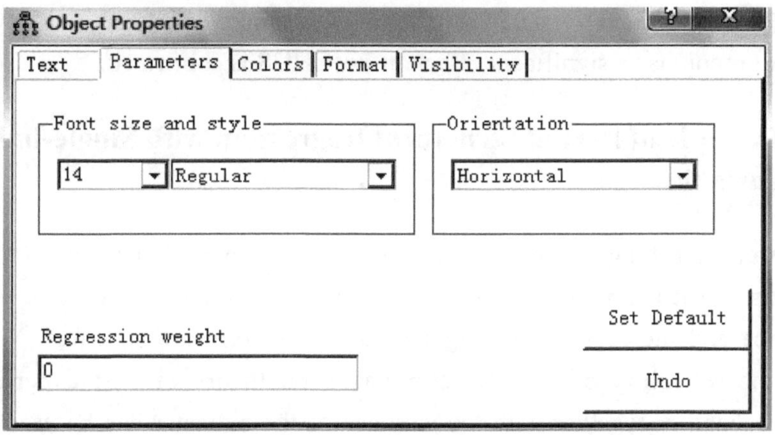

Figure 4.26 Setting the regression weight of PosCHUS on group at 0

Close the box and you will see a model in which the group effect on PosCHUS is set at 0 (Figure 4.27).

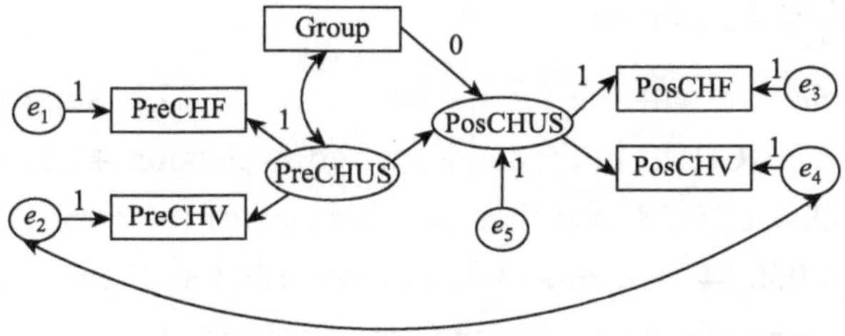

Figure 4.27 A model with the regression weight of PosCHUS on group set at 0

4.2.3.7 Estimation results for the model used for confirmation

Now repeat the analysis, and examine whether the confirmation model is acceptable or not. The selected results are as follows (Table 4.27).

Table 4.27　Summary for the model used for confirmation

Variables	Values
Number of distinct sample moments	15
Number of distinct parameters to be estimated	12
df	3
χ^2	8.639
p	0.034

With $\chi^2 = 8.639$ and $p = 0.034 < 0.05$, the new model is not acceptable. Our initial finding that group has a significant effect on PosCHUS is confirmed.

4.2.4　Example of Partial Structural Regression with Single-indicator Latent Variables

Generally speaking, a latent variable needs two or more indicators to be identified for analysis, but it is possible to have a measurement model with a single indicator if the variance and the regression weight of the error term are specified. We have to estimate the reliability of the indicator based on theory or past experience. The estimated reliability together with the variance of the indicator can be used to further calculate the variance of the error term:

$$\sigma_{\text{err}} = \sigma_{\text{indicator}}(1-\alpha)$$

where $\sigma_{\text{indicator}}$ is the variance of the indicator, and α is the reliability of the indicator. In the following, we will illustrate the application of structural regression analysis with a single-indicator latent variable.

4.2.4.1　Dataset and task

In this example, we will use the dataset in Table 4.22. Suppose PosCHF is the single indicator for PosCHUS in the model tested in Section 4.2.3, with a variance of 0.007 and a reliability of 0.88, and then the variance of the error term for PosCHF is 0.007(1 – 0.88) = 0.000,84. The model can be specified as Figure 4.28. Now we want to estimate the parameters and examine the fitness of this model.

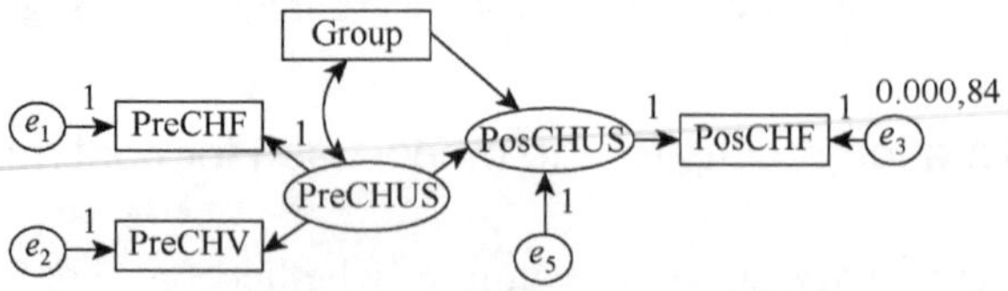

Figure 4.28　A single-indicator model

4.2.4.2 Modeling and results

For the purpose of estimating the parameters and testing the fitness, we have to draw a model in the Amos Graphics window. To fix the variance of the error term of PosCHF at 0.000,84, right click the error term e_3, open the "Object Properties" dialogue box, click the "Parameters" tab, and type "0.000,84" in the "Variance" text box. Close the box and the setting is finished.

Run the analysis for the model created above, and we will get the results. The text output summary is presented in Table 4.28.

Table 4.28 Summary for a single-indicator model

Variables	Values
Number of distinct sample moments	10
Number of distinct parameters to be estimated	9
df	1
χ^2	1.106
p	0.293

The path diagram output is shown below (Figure 4.29). The parameter estimates presented in this model are quite similar to those in the model in Section 4.2.3.5 (see Figure 4.25). For example, the regression weight of PosCHUS on group here is –0.37 (quite similar to –0.36), and the regression weight of PosCHF on PosCHUS is 0.93 (quite similar to 0.94).

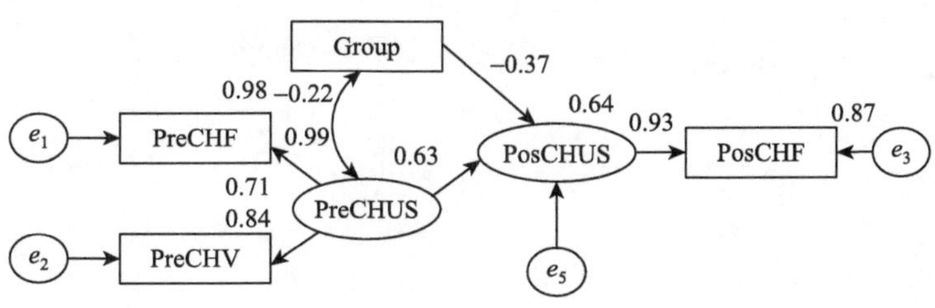

Figure 4.29 Standardized graphic output for a single-indicator model

4.3 Summary

Factor analysis models and structural regression models are similar to path analysis models except that latent variables are involved. In CFA models, the purpose is to examine whether a pre-existing number of factors can explain the relationships among the observed variables. In EFA models, the objective is to identify the number of factors required to account for the relationships among a set of observed variables. EFA is frequently used to develop new models for datasets. Factor analysis models focus on studying the relationships between observed variables and the corresponding factors or latent variables. All those models are very useful in the test or development of theories.

Chapter 5 Data Imputation

In social science research, missing information is not uncommon. In an experiment, a subject may drop out halfway through it. In a survey, a participant may fail to respond to some questions. On such occasions, the researcher will be left with incomplete information related to some individuals involved in the study. Listwise, deletion and pairwise deletion are conventional methods for dealing with incomplete data. These techniques may lead to a reduced sample size, affecting the results. An alternative method is to use the group mean for the missing data. This method adds no new information. It makes no difference in the overall variable mean whether the missing data are replaced or not. Moreover, the standard error is reduced. Amos does not use all those conventional techniques. This chapter is concerned with how Amos deals with missing data.

5.1 Regression Imputation

In regression imputation, ML estimation is used to estimate the parameter values of the model. The parameters of the model are then set at the estimated values. Linear regression analysis is used to predict the missing values from the observed ones. The application is illustrated with the example below.

5.1.1 Dataset and Task

Here is a set of data with missing values (Table 5.1). CET stands for college entrance test score, and WSE for writing self-efficacy (investigated with a questionnaire).

Table 5.1 Dataset with missing values

Number	CET	TTR	WSE
1	113.00	68.50	3.29
2	113.00	70.00	3.43
3	105.00	63.00	

Continued

Number	CET	TTR	WSE
4	116.00	71.00	4.00
5	97.00	48.00	1.93
6	102.00	58.00	2.29
7		60.00	2.71
8	125.00	77.00	4.14
9	105.00	63.00	2.71
10	101.00		2.10
11	123.00	79.00	4.00
12	103.00	60.50	2.29
13	108.00	67.00	
14	110.00	68.50	3.29
15	116.00	70.00	3.71
16	102.00	59.50	2.29
17	101.00	54.30	1.00
18	115.00		3.43
19	97.00	51.00	1.88
20	102.00	62.00	2.71
21	117.00	73.50	
22	101.00	54.50	1.43
23	101.00	57.50	2.14
24	112.00	68.50	3.43
25	107.00	68.00	3.00
26	120.00	76.00	3.71
27	105.00	65.00	2.86
28	104.00	63.00	2.71
29	99.00	53.00	1.89
30	105.00	68.00	2.86

Now we will illustrate how to use regression imputation to impute values for those that are missing.

5.1.2 Procedure for the Data Imputation

From the menus of the Amos Graphics window, select "File" and then "Data Files", and import the incomplete dataset. Build a model with the variables in the dataset, and use the model to estimate the parameters of the variables. A correct over-identified model (a model with positive *df*) can estimate parameters more accurately than a saturated model, but if there is no such a model, a saturated correlation model as follows will do (Figure 5.1).

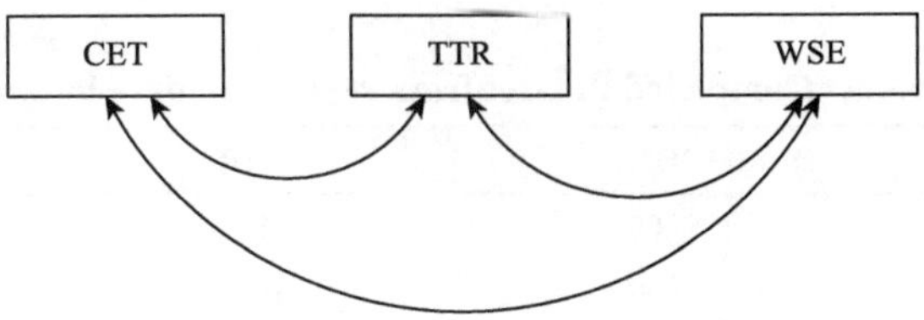

Figure 5.1 A saturated model for data imputation

Select "Estimate means and intercepts" in the "Analysis Properties" dialogue box. This selection is needed for analyses of models with incomplete datasets. Specify the Amos data imputation options in the following steps. First, from the menu, select "Analyze" and then "Amos Data Imputation" (Figure 5.2).

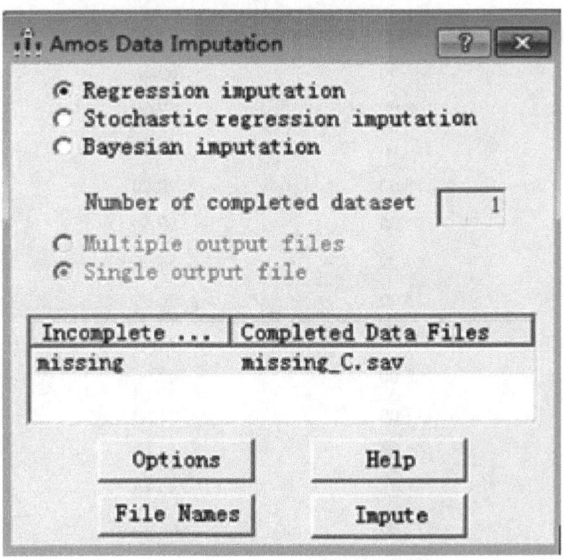

Figure 5.2 Setting for a regression imputation

In the "Amos Data Imputation" dialogue box, select "Regression imputation". Click "File Names" to name the output file. Click "Impute" to produce the completed dataset.

5.1.3 Results for the Data Imputation

The following is the completed data file, which is obtained through the use of regression imputation (Table 5.2).

Table 5.2 Completed dataset from regression data imputation

Number	CET	TTR	WSE
1	113.00	68.50	3.29
2	113.00	70.00	3.43
3	105.00	63.00	2.66
4	116.00	71.00	4.00
5	97.00	48.00	1.93
6	102.00	58.00	2.29
7	104.50	60.00	2.71
8	125.00	77.00	4.14
9	105.00	63.00	2.71
10	101.00	57.35	2.10
11	123.00	79.00	4.00
12	103.00	60.50	2.29
13	108.00	67.00	3.01
14	110.00	68.50	3.29
15	116.00	70.00	3.71
16	102.00	59.50	2.29
17	101.00	54.30	1.00
18	115.00	70.97	3.43
19	97.00	51.00	1.88
20	102.00	62.00	2.71
21	117.00	73.50	3.72
22	101.00	54.50	1.43
23	101.00	57.50	2.14
24	112.00	68.50	3.43
25	107.00	68.00	3.00
26	120.00	76.00	3.71
27	105.00	65.00	2.86
28	104.00	63.00	2.71
29	99.00	53.00	1.89
30	105.00	68.00	2.86

5.2 Stochastic Regression Imputation

Stochastic regression imputation is similar to regression imputation, in which the model parameters are set at the values resulting from ML estimates. The Amos program produces values for the missing observations by randomly drawing from the conditional distribution of the missing observations based on the existing values. Due to the random nature, running the imputation process repeatedly may result in different completed datasets. The dataset in Section 5.1 (see Table 5.1) is to be employed to illustrate the application.

5.2.1 Procedure for the Data Imputation

To use the stochastic regression imputation approach, you have to 1) import the incomplete dataset; 2) build a model with the variables in the dataset, and use the model to estimate the parameters of the variables (Figure 5.1); 3) select "Estimate means and intercepts" in the "Analysis Properties" dialogue box; 4) specify the Amos data imputation options.

We have to go through several steps to complete the specification. From the menus, select "Analyze" and then "Amos Data Imputation". Select "Stochastic regression imputation" in the "Amos Data Imputation" dialogue box. Type "1" in the "Number of completed dataset" text box (the default value of 10 is for multiple imputation). Select "Single output file" ("Multiple output files" are used for multiple imputation, in which the output for each imputation is saved in a separate file) (Figure 5.3).

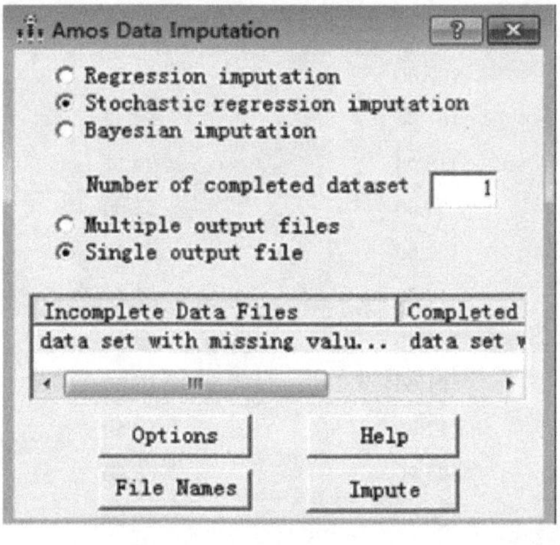

Figure 5.3 Setting for a stochastic regression imputation

Click "File Names" to name the output file. Click "Impute" to produce the completed dataset.

5.2.2 Results for the Data Imputation

The following is the output (Table 5.3). Imputed values here are slightly different from those produced by regression imputation. For example, the TTR for Number 10 is 57.35 based on regression imputation and is 55.17 based on stochastic regression imputation.

Table 5.3 Data from stochastic regression imputation

Number	CET	TTR	WSE
1	113.00	68.50	3.29
2	113.00	70.00	3.43
3	105.00	63.00	2.80
4	116.00	71.00	4.00
5	97.00	48.00	1.93
6	102.00	58.00	2.29
7	104.58	60.00	2.71
8	125.00	77.00	4.14
9	105.00	63.00	2.71
10	101.00	55.17	2.10
11	123.00	79.00	4.00
12	103.00	60.50	2.29
13	108.00	67.00	3.19
14	110.00	68.50	3.29
15	116.00	70.00	3.71
16	102.00	59.50	2.29
17	101.00	54.30	1.00
18	115.00	74.11	3.43
19	97.00	51.00	1.88
20	102.00	62.00	2.71
21	117.00	73.50	3.44
22	101.00	54.50	1.43
23	101.00	57.50	2.14
24	112.00	68.50	3.43
25	107.00	68.00	3.00
26	120.00	76.00	3.71
27	105.00	65.00	2.86

Continued

Number	CET	TTR	WSE
28	104.00	63.00	2.71
29	99.00	53.00	1.89
30	105.00	68.00	2.86

5.3 Bayesian Imputation

Bayesian imputation is similar to stochastic regression imputation except that it uses a different program. The dataset in Section 5.1 (Table 5.1) is to be employed to illustrate the application.

5.3.1 Procedure for the Data Imputation

To perform Bayesian imputation, we have to 1) import the incomplete dataset; 2) build a model with the variables in the dataset, and use the model to estimate the parameters of the variables (see Figure 5.1 in Section 5.1.2); 3) select "Estimate means and intercepts" in the "Analysis Properties" dialogue box; 4) specify the Amos data imputation options.

Several steps are needed to accomplish the specification. From the menu, select "Analyze" and then "Data Imputation". Select "Bayesian imputation" in the "Amos Data Imputation" dialogue box. Type "1" in the "Number of completed dataset" text box (the default value of 10 is for multiple imputation). Select "Single output file" ("Multiple output files" are used for multiple imputation, in which the output for each imputation is saved in a separate file) (Figure 5.4).

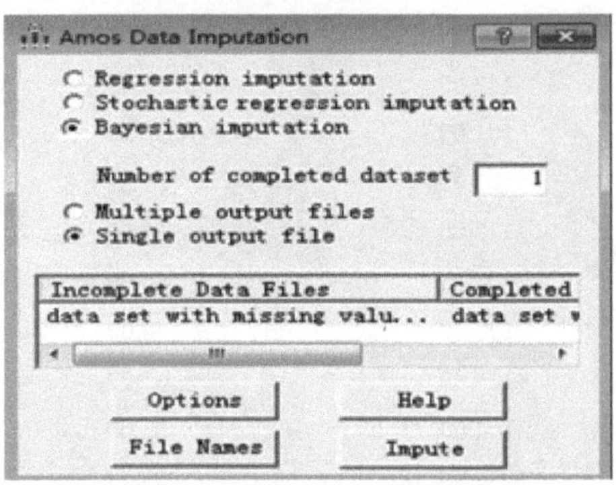

Figure 5.4 Setting for a Bayesian imputation

Click "File Names" to name the output file. Click "Impute" to produce the completed dataset.

5.3.2 Results for the Data Imputation

Here is the completed dataset in an output file (Table 5.4).

Table 5.4 Completed dataset from Bayesian imputation

Number	CET	TTR	WSE
1	113.00	68.50	3.29
2	113.00	70.00	3.43
3	105.00	63.00	2.45
4	116.00	71.00	4.00
5	97.00	48.00	1.93
6	102.00	58.00	2.29
7	103.48	60.00	2.71
8	125.00	77.00	4.14
9	105.00	63.00	2.71
10	101.00	55.23	2.10
11	123.00	79.00	4.00
12	103.00	60.50	2.29
13	108.00	67.00	3.08
14	110.00	68.50	3.29
15	116.00	70.00	3.71
16	102.00	59.50	2.29
17	101.00	54.30	1.00
18	115.00	69.29	3.43
19	97.00	51.00	1.88
20	102.00	62.00	2.71
21	117.00	73.50	3.81
22	101.00	54.50	1.43
23	101.00	57.50	2.14
24	112.00	68.50	3.43
25	107.00	68.00	3.00
26	120.00	76.00	3.71
27	105.00	65.00	2.86
28	104.00	63.00	2.71
29	99.00	53.00	1.89
30	105.00	68.00	2.86

5.4 Multiple Imputation

In multiple imputation, the researcher first employs Bayesian imputation or stochastic regression imputation to produce several datasets, and then one variable is used to predict another in each dataset, which can result in a regression weight for each dataset. After averaging the regression weight from each dataset, the researcher can use the mean weight to predict missing values from the known values in the original dataset. The dataset in Section 5.1 (see Table 5.1) is to be employed to illustrate the application.

5.4.1 Procedure for the Data Imputation

5.4.1.1 Setting the number of completed datasets to be produced

Following the steps introduced in Section 5.3.1, we have to 1) import the incomplete dataset; 2) build a model to estimate the parameters of the variables (see Figure 5.1 in Section 5.1.2); 3) select "Estimate means and intercepts" in the "Analysis Properties" dialogue box; 4) specify the Amos data imputation options. Now we want to use Bayesian imputation to produce three completed datasets saved in multiple files, and the setting is like the following (Figure 5.5).

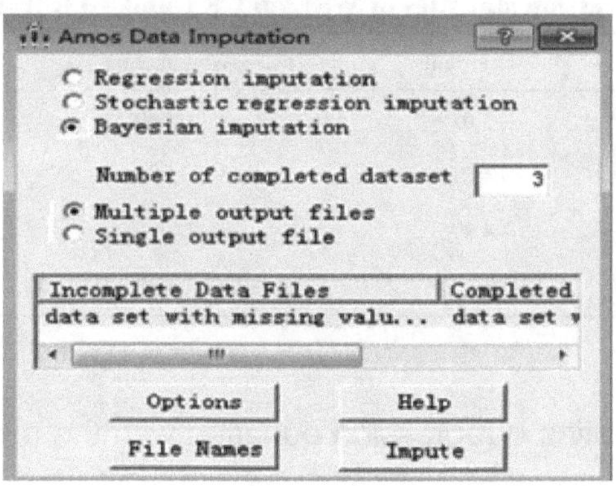

Figure 5.5 Setting for a multiple imputation

5.4.1.2 Producing the desired datasets

When the number of completed datasets is specified, click "Impute" to produce the datasets. Three datasets will be produced. Figure 5.6 displays a section of the first dataset.

	CET	TTR	WSE	CaseNo	ImputeNo
1	113.00	68.50	3.29	1.00	1.00
2	113.00	70.00	3.43	2.00	1.00
3	105.00	63.00	2.57	3.00	1.00
4	116.00	71.00	4.00	4.00	1.00
5	97.00	48.00	1.93	5.00	1.00
6	102.00	58.00	2.29	6.00	1.00
7	107.40	60.00	2.71	7.00	1.00
8	125.00	77.00	4.14	8.00	1.00
9	105.00	63.00	2.71	9.00	1.00
10	101.00	56.43	2.10	10.00	1.00

Figure 5.6 A section of the first dataset produced by Bayesian imputation

5.4.1.3 Analyzing each of the three datasets separately

To analyze the separate files, choose "Analyze" from the "SPSS Statistics" menu. Click "Regression" and "Linear", and perform regression analyses. We have to select one or more variables to predict another. In the present example, we can use CET and TTR to predict WSE. The results are shown in Table 5.5.

Table 5.5 Regression statistics of WSE on CET and TTR from the 3 datasets

Datasets	Constants	Weights on CET	Weights on TTR
1	–5.089	0.040	0.056
2	–4.818	0.035	0.060
3	–4.875	0.039	0.054
Mean	–4.927	0.038	0.056

5.4.1.4 Formulating a regression equation with the means of the constants and weights

With the statistics, we can formulate a combined regression equation, in which WSE regresses on CET and TTR.

$$\mathrm{WSE} = -4.927,3 + 0.038,0 \times \mathrm{CET} + 0.056,7 \times \mathrm{TTR}$$

5.4.2 Results for the Data Imputation

With the combined regression equation above, we can predict the missing values in the original datasets. Table 5.6 displays the completed dataset.

Table 5.6 Completed dataset from multiple imputation

Number	CET	TTR	WSE
1	113.00	68.50	3.29
2	113.00	70.00	3.43
3	105.00	63.00	2.63
4	116.00	71.00	4.00
5	97.00	48.00	1.93
6	102.00	58.00	2.29
7	111.46	60.00	2.71
8	125.00	77.00	4.14
9	105.00	63.00	2.71
10	101.00	56.25	2.10
11	123.00	79.00	4.00
12	103.00	60.50	2.29
13	108.00	67.00	2.98
14	110.00	68.50	3.29
15	116.00	70.00	3.71
16	102.00	59.50	2.29
17	101.00	54.30	1.00
18	115.00	70.32	3.43
19	97.00	51.00	1.88
20	102.00	62.00	2.71
21	117.00	73.50	3.69
22	101.00	54.50	1.43
23	101.00	57.50	2.14
24	112.00	68.50	3.43
25	107.00	68.00	3.00
26	120.00	76.00	3.71
27	105.00	65.00	2.86
28	104.00	63.00	2.71
29	99.00	53.00	1.89
30	105.00	68.00	2.86

In fact, different data imputation methods have been found to be capable of producing similar results for missing values. For example, the WSE of Number 21 is 3.69 in Table 5.6, 3.81 in Table 5.4, 3.44 in Table 5.3, and 3.72 in Table 5.2.

5.5 Summary

Data imputation is required when we are faced with incomplete datasets. Means and intercepts are to be estimated before the imputation is conducted. In regression data imputation, a correct over-identified model is preferable to a saturated model. Stochastic regression imputation is similar to general regression imputation except that the Amos program generates values for the missing data by randomly drawing from the conditional distribution of the missing data based on the available data. Bayesian imputation is similar to stochastic regression imputation except that a different program is involved in the estimation. Multiple imputation uses Bayesian imputation or stochastic regression imputation to generate several datasets. Then one variable is used to predict another in order to produce a regression weight for each dataset. When the regression weights from different datasets are averaged, the researcher can use the mean weight to form a regression equation for the prediction of missing observations.

Chapter 6 Analyses with Censored and Ordered-Category Data

Censored data are data which record only part of the variation of a variable. Ordered-category data are values of ordered-category variables. Bayesian estimation has to be employed for models involving censored data or ordered-category data. In this chapter, the applications are introduced respectively.

6.1 Analyses with Censored Data

Due to the capacity of the measurement instruments or other incidents, for some observations, values beyond a certain point are not recorded. For example, on a word association test, a group of students are required to produce as many words related to "book" as possible. John produced 10 words, Kate produced 15, and Rose produced 30 before she was stopped by the teacher. The number of words produced by John and Kate are uncensored, but the number by Rose is censored. Without the interruption of the teacher, Rose could have produced more words. There are two types of frequently seen censored data, namely left censored data and right censored data. For left censored data, values below a certain point are not recorded; for right censored data, values above a certain point are not recorded. Censored variables are assumed to be in normal distribution. Bayesian estimation has to be employed for models involving censored data.

6.1.1 Dataset and Task

Here is an example for demonstrating the analysis of censored data. The sample was 30 students who received tests on their English writing and vocabulary decoding (DEC). The lexical variation (LV) and complex T-unit ratio (a complex T-unit ratio is the number of complex T-units divided by the total number of T-units, as labeled by "CTtoT") of the writing were calculated with the Lexical Complexity Analyzer and Syntactic Analyzer. Decoding was measured by the number of vocabulary correctly decoded. The test ended if 1) a student incorrectly decoded 5 words in succession, or 2) when 3 minutes were over. If a student's test was ended by the time limit, we are sure that the student can get a higher score if given enough time. But we cannot find out exactly how many points he or she could get. The possible higher score is not recorded or is censored. The data are displayed in Table 6.1.

Table 6.1 Censored data to be analyzed

Number	LV	CTtoT	DEC
1	0.57	0.60	74.00
2	0.61	0.62	72.00
3	0.53	0.57	71.00
4	0.41	0.52	72.00
5	0.55	0.59	74.00
6	0.71	0.67	74.00
7	0.58	0.59	71.00
8	0.69	0.81	>90.00
9	0.59	0.62	75.00
10	0.63	0.70	74.00
11	0.69	0.74	87.00
12	0.52	0.57	73.00
13	0.77	0.79	96.00
14	0.59	0.59	70.00
15	0.57	0.59	72.00
16	0.74	0.83	>97.00
17	0.61	0.69	74.00
18	0.54	0.57	71.00
19	0.74	0.65	>95.00
20	0.72	0.79	88.00
21	0.57	0.59	71.00
22	0.61	0.64	77.00
23	0.69	0.77	91.00
24	0.54	0.57	70.00
25	0.59	0.61	74.00
26	0.57	0.69	76.00
27	0.53	0.57	71.00
28	0.51	0.56	71.00
29	0.67	0.76	76.00
30	0.74	0.80	>93.00

Now we want to estimate the regression of decoding on lexical variation and complex T-unit ratio (Figure 6.1).

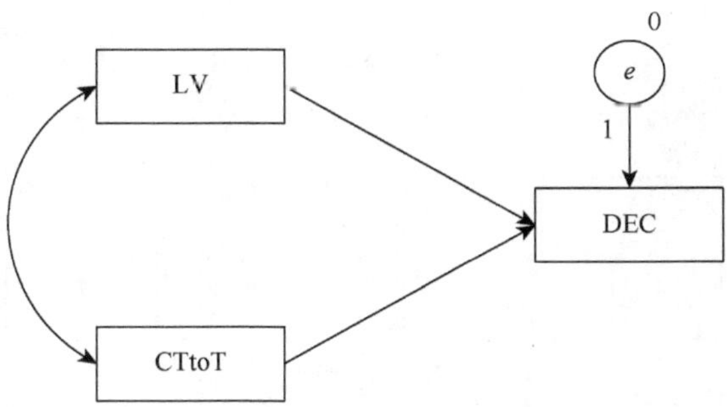

Figure 6.1 Regression of decoding on lexical variation and complex T-unit ratio

6.1.2 Procedure for the Task

6.1.2.1 Modeling with Amos Graphics

A. Processing the censored data as strings in SPSS

We have to recode the data before they are imported to Amos. The variables involving censored data should be processed as strings in SPSS. In this example, only the variable DEC has censored values, and has to be processed as strings (Figure 6.2).

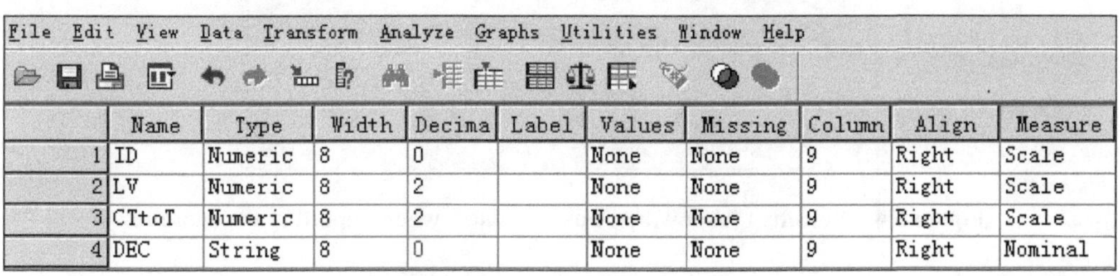

	Name	Type	Width	Decima	Label	Values	Missing	Column	Align	Measure
1	ID	Numeric	8	0		None	None	9	Right	Scale
2	LV	Numeric	8	2		None	None	9	Right	Scale
3	CTtoT	Numeric	8	2		None	None	9	Right	Scale
4	DEC	String	8	0		None	None	9	Right	Nominal

Figure 6.2 Selecting strings for data type for the censored variable

The symbol ">" should be placed before right censored values, indicating that the actual values are larger than the recorded ones (Figure 6.3).

	ID	LV	CTtoT	DEC
2	2	0.61	0.62	72
3	3	0.53	0.57	71
4	4	0.41	0.52	72
5	5	0.55	0.59	74
6	6	0.71	0.67	74
7	7	0.58	0.59	71
8	8	0.69	0.81	>90
9	9	0.59	0.62	75
10	10	0.63	0.70	74
11	11	0.69	0.74	87
12	12	0.52	0.57	73
13	13	0.77	0.79	96
14	14	0.59	0.59	70
15	15	0.57	0.59	72
16	16	0.74	0.83	>97
17	17	0.61	0.69	74
18	18	0.54	0.57	71
19	19	0.74	0.65	>95
20	20	0.72	0.79	88

Figure 6.3 Recoding the censored data

B. Importing the data file to Amos

Import the processed data file to Amos, and select "Allow non-numeric data" (Figure 6.4).

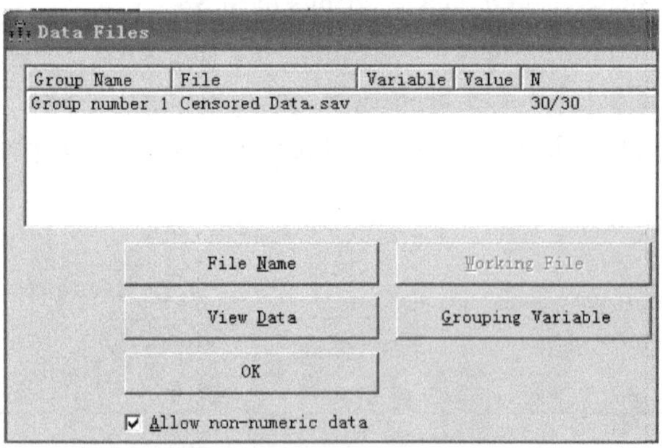

Figure 6.4 Selecting "Allow non-numeric data" when importing the data file

C. Building the path diagram and running the analysis

To analyze censored data, we have to reproduce a path diagram similar to the model to be tested. When the model is drawn, select "Estimate means and intercepts" in the "Analysis Properties" dialogue box. In the Amos tool area, click the button, or click "Analyze" and then "Bayesian Estimation". The Bayesian estimation will start at once. The estimation may take some time before convergence is attained. When it is, the ● becomes ☺. Click the pause button ❚❚ on the tool bar, and the estimation will be terminated. We can examine the text results.

6.1.2.2 Summary of the posterior distribution and the fitness measures

Table 6.2 is a summary of the posterior distribution of each parameter. Here we can see the mean, standard error (S.E.), standard deviation (S.D.), convergence statistic (C.S.), and the minimum (Min) and maximum (Max) values of the parameters.

Table 6.2 Posterior distribution of each parameter

Parameters	Mean	S.E.	S.D.	C.S.	Min	Max
Regression weights						
DEC<--LV	48.557	0.163	27.963	1.000	−102.801	202.083
DEC<--CTtoT	50.841	0.155	27.005	1.000	−78.121	201.965
Means						
LV	0.613	0.000	0.018	1.000	0.528	0.705
CTtoT	0.655	0.000	0.019	1.000	0.577	0.749
Intercepts						
DEC	15.444	0.051	8.774	1.000	−38.126	60.259
Covariances						
LV<->CTtoT	0.009	0.000	0.003	1.000	0.003	0.037
Variances						
LV	0.009	0.000	0.003	1.000	0.003	0.035
CTtoT	0.010	0.000	0.003	1.000	0.004	0.040
e	36.061	0.137	13.095	1.000	9.706	148.002

Based on Bayesian estimation, each parameter is not a fixed value, but a distribution. In Table 6.2, each row presents the summary of the posterior distribution of a parameter.

In the "Bayesian SEM" window, click "View" and "Fitness Measure", and we can examine the p value. In this example, $p = 0.42 > 0.05$, indicating that the model tested is plausible. This posterior predictive p can be regarded as the posterior mean of a conventional p value.

6.1.2.3 Polygon plots of posterior distribution

Right-click a row which contains a parameter, select "Show Posterior" from the pop-up menu, and the distribution plot will be displayed. For example, if we right-click the regression weight of DEC on LV, we will see the following (Figure 6.5).

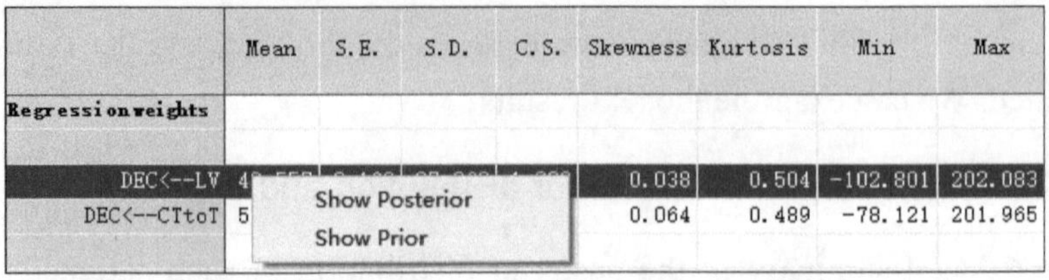

Figure 6.5 Selection for viewing the distribution plot

Further click "Show Posterior", and we can see the polygon plot on the distribution of the regression weight of DEC on LV (Figure 6.6).

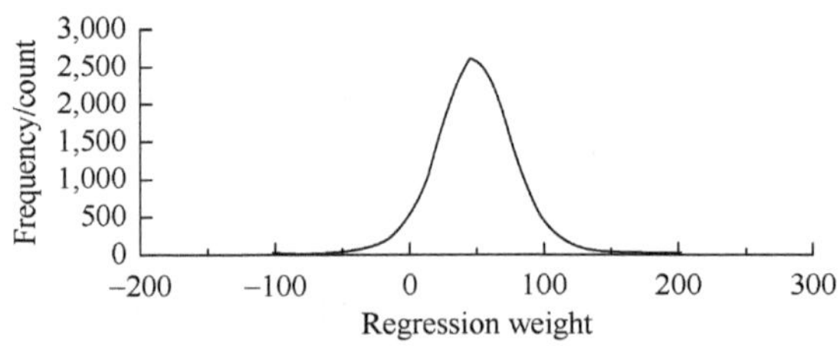

Figure 6.6 Distribution of the regression weight of DEC on LV

Notes: Regression weight refers to estimated regression weight in a distribution around the mean (applicable to Figure 6.7); frequency refers to frequency count of each estimated regression weight (applicable to Figure 6.7)

The mean 48.557 in Table 6.2 falls approximately at the midpoint of the distribution curve, which suggests that most of the regression weights are around the mean. The curve also shows that weights around the mean have a high frequency. The minimum value −102.801 corresponds to the left end of the curve, while the maximum value 202.083 corresponds to the right end of the curve. The curve further suggests that most of the estimated repression weights fall between 0 and 100. Figure 6.7 is the posterior distribution of DEC on CTtoT. The regression weights also cluster around the mean 50.841 (Table 6.2).

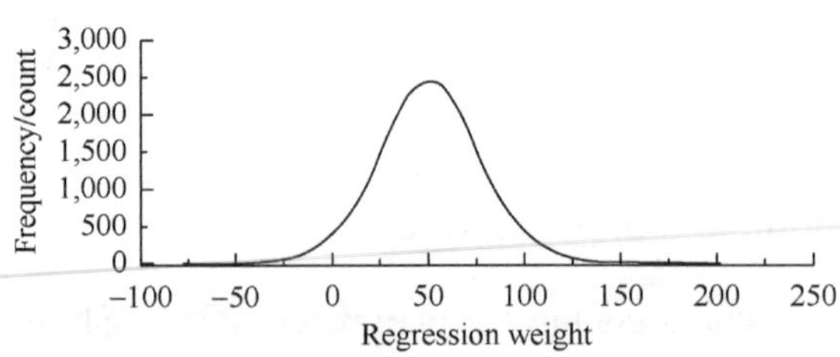

Figure 6.7 Distribution of the regression weight of DEC on CTtoT

6.1.2.4 Posterior predictive distribution

In the “Bayesian SEM” window, click (“View” → “Posterior Predictive”), and we can see a table with “<<” standing for the censored observation (Figure 6.8).

The first column is the students’ ID. The other numbers in the window are the non-censored values. Each “<<” stands for a censored value. Double-click a “<<”, and we can see the posterior predictive distribution of the censored score. For example, for the student with the ID of 8 (S8), the DEC is a censored value (>90), as is symbolized by a “<<” here. Double-click the “<<”, and we can see that the DEC score has the highest probability (frequency) of being 90 points, and that as the value increases, the probability decreases steadily (Figure 6.9). The highest score does not exceed 112.5 points.

	LV	CTtoT	DEC
1	0.57	0.6	74
2	0.61	0.62	72
3	0.53	0.57	71
4	0.41	0.52	72
5	0.55	0.59	74
6	0.71	0.67	74
7	0.58	0.50	71
8	0.69	0.81	<<
9	0.59	0.62	75
10	0.63	0.7	74
11	0.69	0.74	87
12	0.52	0.57	73
13	0.77	0.79	96
14	0.59	0.59	70
15	0.57	0.59	72
16	0.74	0.83	<<

Figure 6.8 Viewing the posterior predictive distribution

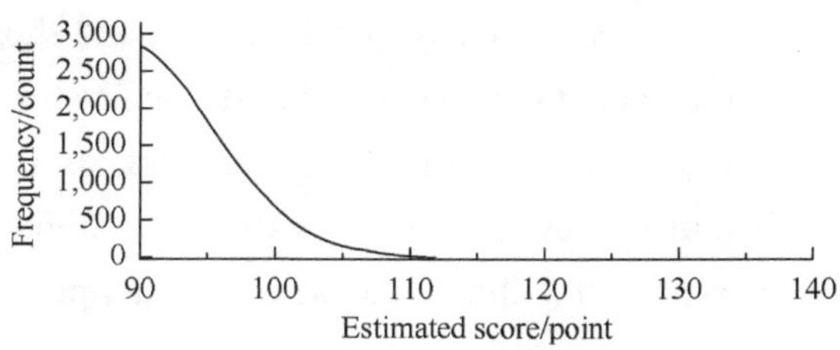

Figure 6.9 Posterior predictive distribution of the censored score “>90”

Notes: Estimated score refers to estimated score distribution for the censored score “>90” (applicable to Figure 6.10); frequency refers to frequency count of each estimated score (applicable to Figure 6.10)

Figure 6.10 is the predictive distribution of DEC of the student with the ID of 16 (S16, with a censored score of “>97”). Compared with S8, S16 is more likely to have a

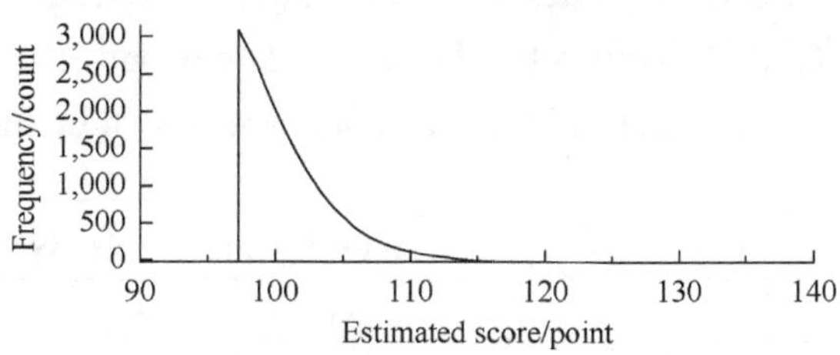

Figure 6.10 Posterior predictive distribution of the censored score “>97”

higher score, with a high probability (frequency) of getting 97 points. The highest score approaches 115 points.

6.2 Analyses with Ordered-Category Data

Ordered-category data are values of ordered-category variables. An ordered-category variable is used to classify things, individuals or characteristics into a limited number of levels. Ordered-category data are widely used in applied linguistics. For example, to assess the language performance of the students, a teacher may rate students as A (excellent), B (good), and C (poor). The thesis examination committee may use P (pass) and F (fail) to evaluate students' graduation papers. The response choices to Likert scale, strictly speaking, are ordered-category data (e.g. the question "I am afraid to speak English in the English class." may be followed by response choices, such as strongly disagree, disagree, undecided, agree, and strongly agree). Sometimes, we may transform numerical data into ordered-categorical ones according to predetermined cut-points. For example, the mean length of sentences (MLS) may be labeled as long (if MLS$\geqslant$20), medium (if 10 < MLS < 20), and short (if MLS$\leqslant$10).

The intervals between adjacent choices on a questionnaire (or rating scale) are not necessarily equal. To convert the categories into numbers, as is practiced by many researchers, may be inappropriate. Amos provides a method for analyzing the categories directly. The application is illustrated with the example below.

6.2.1 Dataset and Task

A sample of 103 university students was involved in the study. Each was required to write an essay. Lexical Complexity Analyzer was employed to calculate the adjective variation (ADJV), adverb variation (ADVV), and modifier variation (MODV) of each essay. The numerical values for each index were transformed into ordered-category data (A, B, C, D, E, with A for the lowest degree and E for the highest degree) according to specific cut-points (omitted). The data are shown in Table 6.3.

Table 6.3 Ordered-category data for lexical complexity indices

Number	Letters for values		
	ADJV	ADVV	MODV
1	B	B	C
2	D	B	B

Continued

Number	Letters for values		
	ADJV	ADVV	MODV
3	B	D	D
4	D	A	C
5	B	B	D
6	B	A	D
7	B	D	C
8	A	E	C
9	D	C	B
10	B	C	D
11	C	B	B
12	B	B	C
13	C	C	C
14	D	B	D
15	B	B	B
16	B	C	D
17	C	C	C
18	C	B	C
19	B	D	D
20	D	B	C
21	D	B	B
22	B	B	D
23	B	B	D
24	D	B	C
25	D	A	C
26	C	C	C
27	D	B	C
28	B	B	B
29	B	A	B
30	B	D	C
31	D	A	B
32	C	B	B
33	B	D	D
34	C	B	D
35	C	B	C
36	C	B	D
37	B	B	C
38	A	D	B

Continued

Number	Letters for values		
	ADJV	ADVV	MODV
39	D	B	D
40	D	B	D
41	B	C	D
42	D	B	B
43	B	B	C
44	B	D	D
45	C	B	C
46	C	B	C
47	C	B	B
48	C	B	C
49	C	C	C
50	B	B	D
51	B	D	C
52	C	C	C
53	D	B	D
54	B	C	C
55	C	B	D
56	B	D	C
57	B	B	C
58	D	A	A
59	D	B	C
60	B	B	B
61	A	C	C
62	D	B	B
63	B	B	B
64	B	B	B
65	C	B	B
66	A	B	B
67	B	B	C
68	C	D	B
69	D	B	B
70	B	B	B
71	B	B	B
72	B	D	D
73	B	D	B

Continued

Number	Letters for values		
	ADJV	ADVV	MODV
74	B	D	D
75	A	B	D
76	A	A	C
77	D	A	B
78	C	D	D
79	B	D	D
80	D	B	B
81	A	E	E
82	B	D	C
83	B	B	B
84	B	B	B
85	D	A	B
86	C	B	D
87	B	E	E
88	B	D	C
89	D	B	C
90	D	B	C
91	C	B	B
92	B	D	E
93	B	D	D
94	B	C	D
95	D	B	B
96	C	C	C
97	C	C	D
98	B	B	C
99	D	B	C
100	B	B	B
101	B	D	D
102	B	C	D
103	B	B	B

In this example, we will examine a model in which ADJV has direct effects on ADVV, while ADVV has direct effects on MODV. Since we have to use Bayesian estimation, means and intercepts need to be estimated (Figure 6.11).

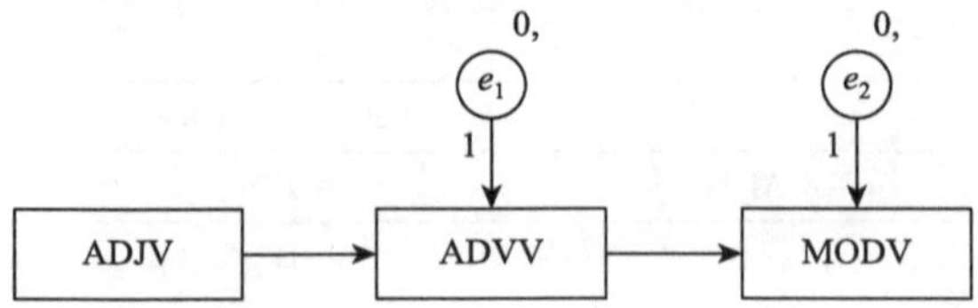

Figure 6.11 Model for ordered-category data

6.2.2 Procedure for the Task

6.2.2.1 Modeling with Amos Graphics

A. Processing the data as strings in SPSS

To accomplish the analysis, we have to process the data as strings in SPSS. The data type should be specified as strings (Figure 6.12).

	Name	Type	Width	Decimals
1	ADJV	String	8	0
2	ADVV	String	8	0
3	MODV	String	8	0

Figure 6.12 Data type specified as strings in SPSS

B. Importing the data file to Amos

Before further setting is performed, we have to import the data files to Amos. In the "Data Files" dialogue box, select "Allow non-numeric data" (Figure 6.13). Click "OK" to close the box.

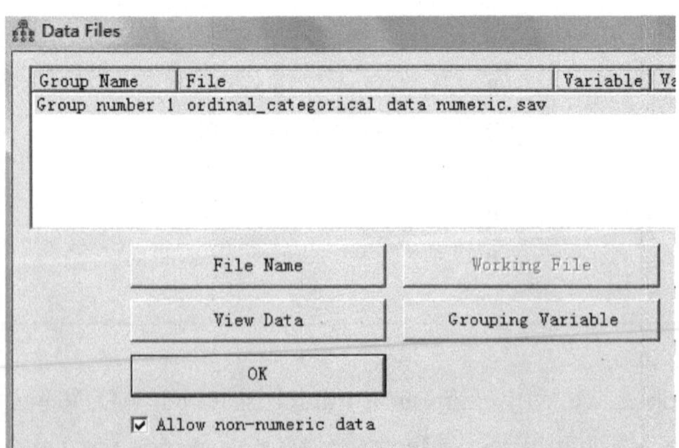

Figure 6.13 Selecting "Allow non-numeric data" when importing the data

C. Building the path diagram

Build a path diagram like Figure 6.11 in the drawing area of Amos Graphics window. Select “Estimate means and intercepts” in the “Analysis Properties” dialogue box.

6.2.2.2 Recoding and analyzing the data

Several steps are needed for the data recoding. From the menus, select “Tools” and then “Data Recode”. In the “Data Recode” window, select the first variable to be recoded (Figure 6.14).

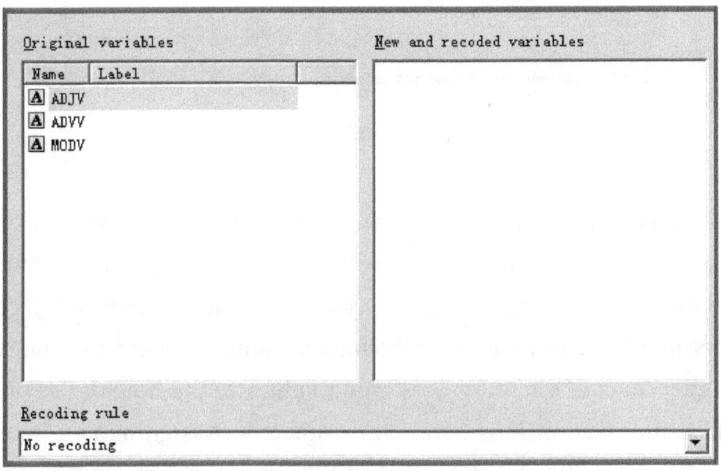

Figure 6.14 Selecting the variable to be recoded

Click “No recoding”, and you will see a dropdown list. From the list, select “Ordered-categorical” (Figure 6.15). In the lower left corner of the window, you can see the frequency of each original value.

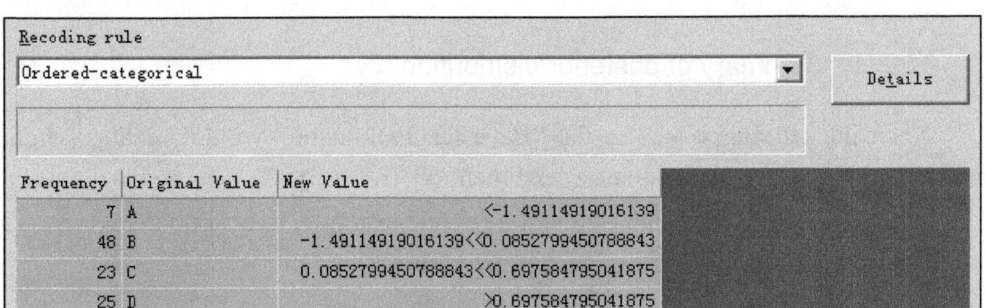

Figure 6.15 Selecting “Order-categorical” as the recoding rule

Click "Details" and open the "Ordered-Categorical Details" dialogue box. Click the first boundary, and type "1" in the text box. Click the second boundary, and type "2" in the text box (Figure 6.16).

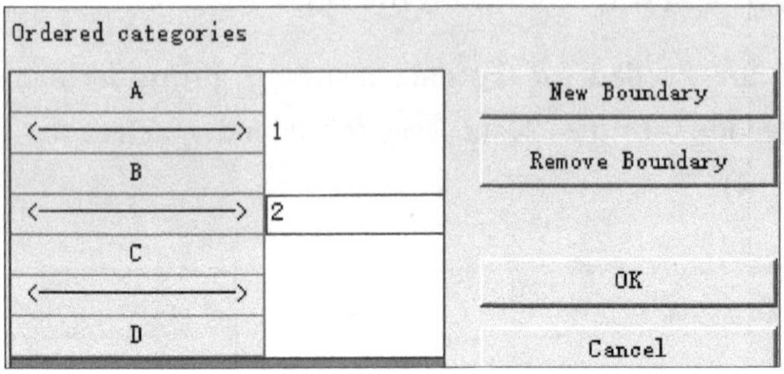

Figure 6.16 Specifying boundary values for ADJV

Here are some notes for choosing values for boundaries. We can trust Amos to estimate all the boundary values, or specify one or two boundary values, and trust Amos to estimate all the other boundary values, no matter how many categories are involved. Any number can be used as boundary values so long as a larger number is used for a higher level of category. Assigning values to the boundaries does not affect the model fit or the relationships between parameters. Assigning two boundary values can help Amos to calculate the zero point and the measurement unit for the underlying continuous variable. In the present example, we can choose "1" and "2", and specify the boundary values for other variables in similar ways. Then close the "Data Recode" window and run the analysis (Bayesian SEM).

6.2.3 Estimation Results

6.2.3.1 Summary of posterior distribution

When the red angry face in the "Bayesian Estimation" window changes into a yellow smiling face, click ⏸ (pause) and then (refresh). We can see the number of iterations taken by the Bayesian estimation (in this example, it is 5,000 iterations). The summary of the posterior distribution appears (Table 6.4).

Table 6.4 Posterior distribution by Bayesian estimation

Parameters	Mean	S.E.	S.D.	C.S.	Min	Max
Regressions						
ADVV<--ADJV	−0.466	0.002	0.101	1.000	−0.868	−0.128
MODV<--ADVV	0.462	0.003	0.097	1.001	0.119	0.833
Mean						
ADJV	1.952	0.002	0.070	1.000	1.671	2.214
Intercepts						
ADVV	2.708	0.004	0.202	1.000	1.976	3.491
MODV	1.418	0.005	0.184	1.000	0.740	2.129
Variances						
ADJV	0.450	0.004	0.090	1.001	0.231	0.859
e_1	0.286	0.002	0.054	1.001	0.153	0.527
e_2	0.227	0.001	0.045	1.000	0.104	0.408

In the summary table, the posterior distribution of two regression weights (ADVV on ADJV and MODV on ADVV), one mean (ADJV), two intercepts (ADVV and MODV), and three variances (ADJV, e_1 and e_2) are displayed. The largest C.S. less than 1.002 is generally accepted as an indicator of convergence of the procedure.

6.2.3.2 Fitness measure

In the "Bayesian SEM" window, click "View" and then "Fitness Measure", and we can see the p value. With $p = 0.53 > 0.05$, the present model is acceptable.

6.2.3.3 Polygon plots of posterior distribution

From the menus of the "Bayesian SEM" window, click "View" and then "Posterior". Select a parameter, select "Polygon", and you can see the polygon plots of posterior distribution of the estimates of the parameter. The following is the distribution for the regression weight of MODV on ADVV (Figure 6.17). Consistent with the mean of

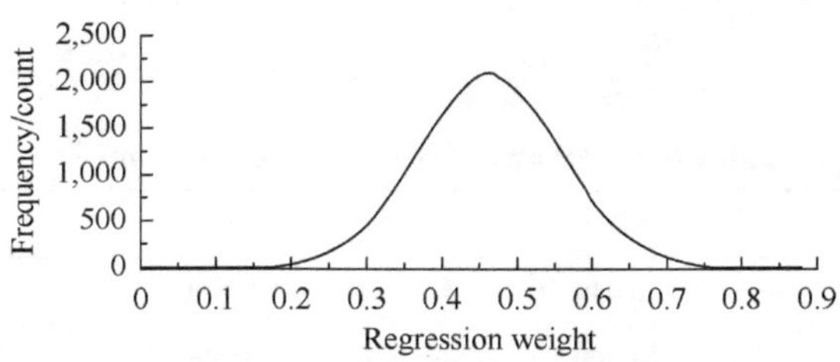

Figure 6.17 Distribution of the regression weight of MODV on ADVV

0.462 shown in Table 6.4, the regression weights around that value have relatively high frequencies.

6.2.3.4 Correlation plots of posterior distribution

In the "Posterior" window, if we click the "Autocorrelation", we can observe the correlation plot (Figure 6.18). It is the correlation of the sampled value at any iteration to another sampled value k iterations later ($k = 1, 2, 3, \cdots$). The plot shows how long it needs for the correlations among samples to die down. The correlation approaching 0 suggests that the samples analyzed are really from posterior distribution. In the current analysis, the autocorrelation plot suggests that less than 5 iterations are enough for the correlation to die down.

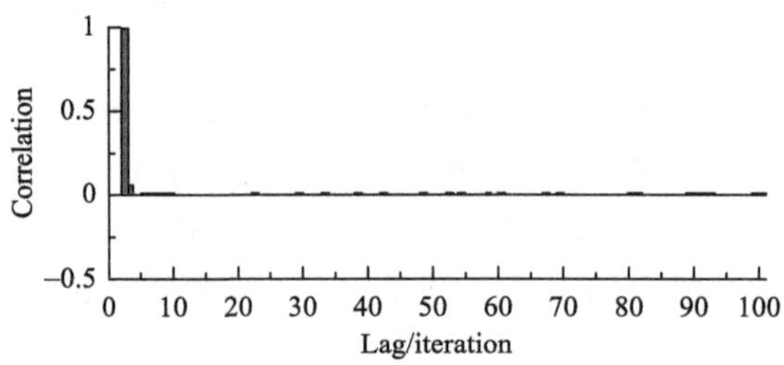

Figure 6.18 Autocorrelation plot for the regression of MODV on ADVV

Notes: Lag refers to the number of iterations between two correlated sample values; correlation refers to correlation coefficient corresponding to a lag

The quick and sudden drop of the autocorrelation suggests that the convergence occurs much soon.

6.2.3.5 Additional estimands

In the "Bayesian SEM" window, click "View" and then "Additional estimands", and you can examine other estimates. Table 6.5 shows the means of the implied covariances.

Table 6.5 Means of the implied covariances

Variables	ADJV	ADVV	MODV
ADJV	0.449	−0.209	−0.096
ADVV	−0.209	0.386	0.178
MODV	−0.096	0.178	0.311

6.3 Summary

Bayesian estimation is the method applicable to the analysis of censored and ordered-category data. To study censored data, the variables with censored data have to be processed as strings in SPSS. When importing the data, we have to instruct Amos that non-numerical data are allowed. The means and intercepts have to be estimated. The results include a summary of the posterior distribution of each parameter, and various plots corresponding to the parameter distributions and estimations. By viewing the posterior predictive distribution, we can see distribution of the predicted values for a censored datum. When analyzing ordered-category data, we have processed the data as strings, and instruct Amos that non-numerical data are to be allowed. Boundary values have to be specified between the categories. The results are similar to those for censored data analysis.

Chapter 7 Bootstrapping

Bootstrapping is a statistical technique which uses the original sample as a population, and produces new samples (bootstrap samples) by sampling with replacement from the original one. This technique can be used to compare the fit of two (or more) competing models, or to compare the appropriateness of different estimation methods.

7.1 Bootstrapping Used in Model Comparison

Bootstrapping can be used for the comparison of competing models. To select the best model, bootstrapping program first produces a large number of bootstrap samples. Then it tests each model with each of the bootstrap samples. All the discrepancies between the implied moments of the bootstrap samples and that of the population are computed and averaged. The model with the smallest mean of discrepancy is selected as the best model. The application is illustrated with the example below.

7.1.1 Dataset and Task

Here is an example, which involves 30 university participants. Data on CET, TTR of speaking performance of the first term test (FTT), TTR of speaking performance of the second term test (STT), and SSE were collected (Table 7.1).

Table 7.1 Data for CET, FTT, STT and SSE

Number	CET	FTT	STT	SSE
1	95.00	66.00	68.00	1.71
2	103.00	71.00	75.00	2.29
3	118.00	88.00	84.00	3.29
4	108.00	79.00	78.00	2.71
5	120.00	76.00	73.00	3.43
6	110.00	79.00	75.00	2.71

Continued

Number	CET	FTT	STT	SSE
7	120.00	79.00	76.00	3.43
8	108.00	77.00	78.00	2.71
9	118.00	87.00	86.00	3.00
10	110.00	80.00	85.00	2.71
11	113.00	80.00	78.00	2.86
12	117.00	71.00	74.00	4.00
13	111.00	81.00	83.00	2.71
14	113.00	85.00	85.00	2.86
15	98.00	69.00	67.00	2.29
16	116.00	91.00	94.00	3.00
17	88.00	57.00	59.00	1.00
18	114.00	79.00	77.00	3.00
19	112.00	83.00	88.00	3.20
20	109.00	81.00	76.00	3.29
21	109.00	82.00	75.00	2.71
22	107.00	85.00	85.00	3.29
23	114.00	76.00	65.00	3.43
24	115.00	87.00	81.00	2.86
25	115.00	86.00	83.00	3.43
26	108.00	78.00	78.00	3.71
27	112.00	79.00	74.00	3.71
28	116.00	81.00	75.00	4.00
29	113.00	79.00	73.00	4.14
30	92.00	63.00	70.00	1.43

Now we will use CET, FTT and STT to predict SSE. This involves a regression analysis. Five models are to be compared with the bootstrap approach (Figure 7.1 to Figure 7.5).

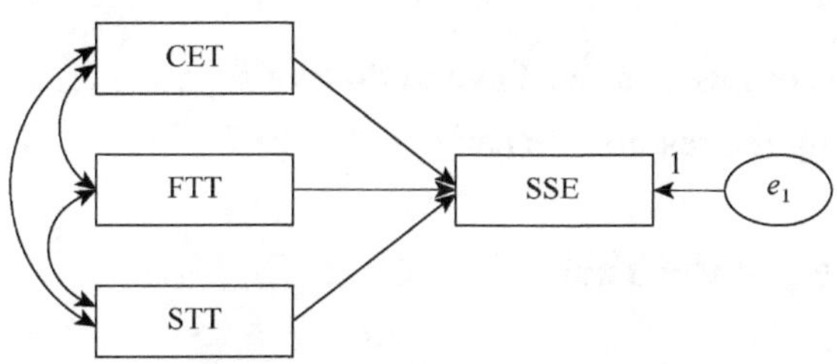

Figure 7.1 Competing Model A

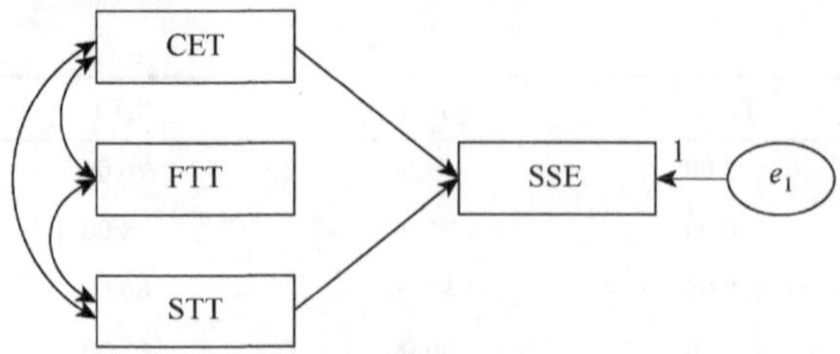

Figure 7.2 Competing Model B

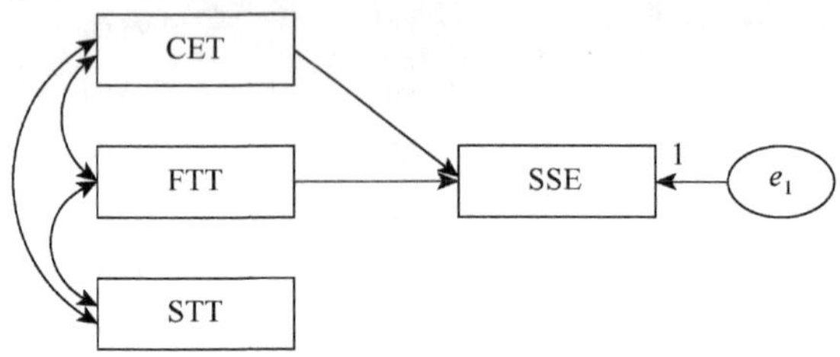

Figure 7.3 Competing Model C

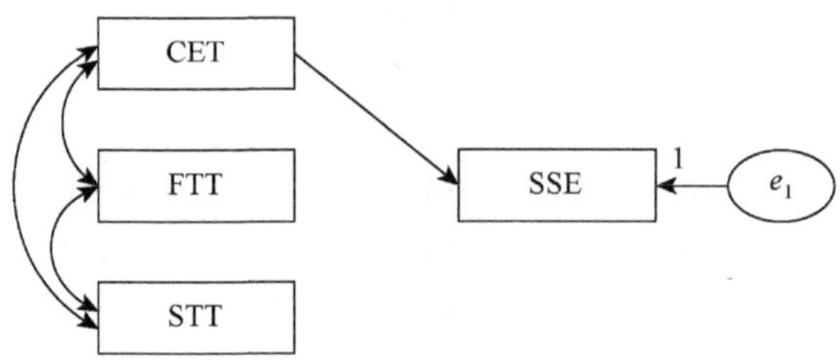

Figure 7.4 Competing Model D

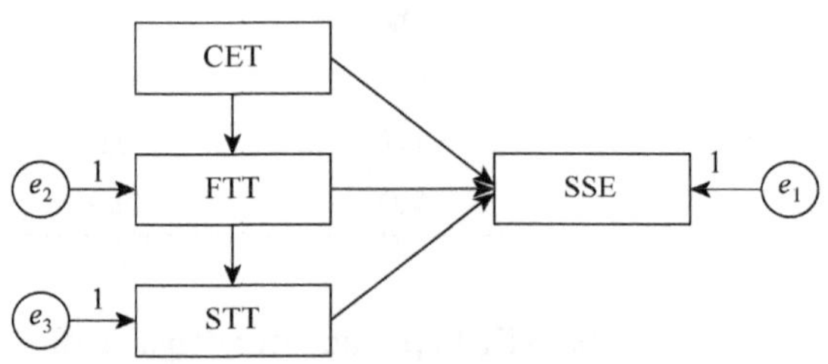

Figure 7.5 Competing Model E

To perform the comparison, we have to do five separate analyses with each of the models. By comparing the results, we can decide which model is the best.

7.1.2 Procedure for the Task

Here are the key steps. The steps should be followed for each of the five analyses.

First, import the well-processed data to Amos Graphics. Second, build the input path diagram in the drawing area of the Amos Graphics window. Third, set the analysis properties. To accomplish the setting, we have to 1) open "Analysis Properties" dialogue box; 2) click the "Bootstrap" tab and select "Perform bootstrap"; 3) type "1,000" in the text box near the "Number of bootstrap samples" (Figure 7.6); 4) select the "Random #" tab, and type "1" or any other number in the text box near the "Seed for random numbers" (the same seed must be used in order to let Amos draw the same samples for testing the model) (Figure 7.7); 5) click the "Numerical" tab, and type "50" (or any other practical number) in the "Iteration limit" text box (here 50 suggests that after 50 iterations, the calculation will stop) (Figure 7.8); 6) close the box and run the analysis.

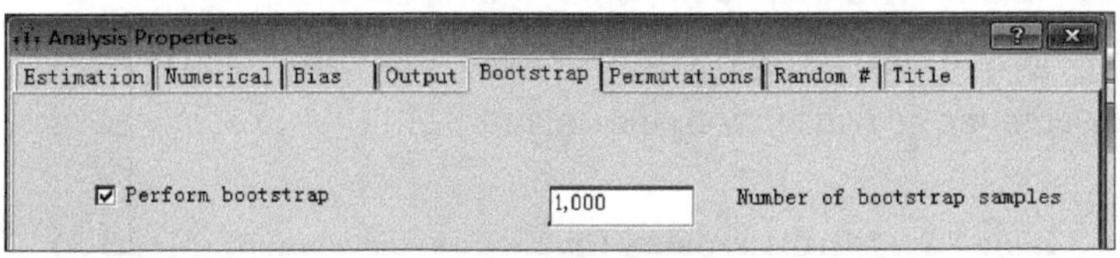

Figure 7.6 Setting the bootstrap options

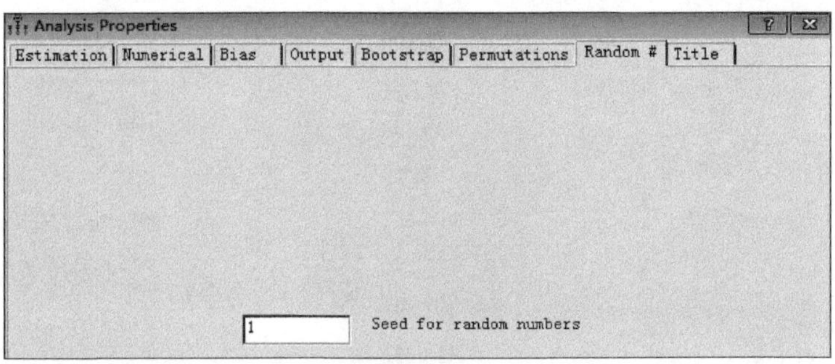

Figure 7.7 Setting the seed for random numbers

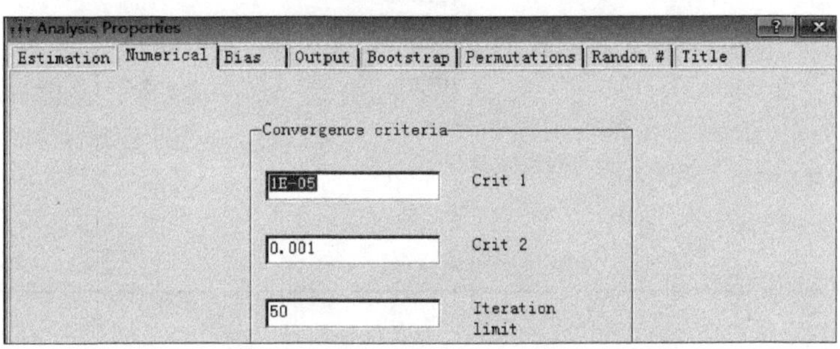

Figure 7.8 Setting the iteration limit

7.1.3 Output for the Analysis

The following are the results selected from each analysis for comparison.

In the navigation tree for text output, click "Summary of Bootstrap Iterations", you can see that 0 bootstrap sample was unused because of a singular covariance matrix; 0 bootstrap sample was unused because a solution was not found; 1,000 usable bootstrap samples were obtained.

The message suggests that all the 1,000 bootstrap samples were employed in the analysis. If there are *n* samples unused for a certain model, we should increase the number of bootstrap samples by *n*, and repeat the analysis for the model so that the results are comparable with other competing model results.

In the navigation tree for text output, click "Bootstrap distribution", and you will see the ML discrepancy (distribution, mean, and S.E.) (Table 7.2).

Table 7.2 ML discrepancy (implied vs. population) (Model A)

Summary	Discrepancy	Distribution
	…	…
	2.160	|**********
	18.783	|********************
	35.406	|*******
	52.029	|***
	68.652	|**
	85.275	|*
	101.899	|*
N = 1,000 Mean = 23.872 S.E. = 0.702	118.522	|*
	135.145	|*
	151.768	|
	168.391	|
	185.014	|*
	201.637	|
	218.261	|
	234.884	|*
	…	…

The mean of discrepancies between the moments of the bootstrap population (original sample) and the implied moments (got from fitting the model to each of the 1,000 bootstrap samples) was 23.872, and the S.E. was 0.702.

The ML discrepancies (implied vs. population) for Models B, C, D and E are omitted here. But the mean and S.E. are displayed in Table 7.3.

Table 7.3 Mean and S.E. of ML discrepancy of each model

Models	Mean	S.E.
A	23.872	0.702
B	21.333	0.637
C	23.256	0.677
D	21.071	0.580
E	24.434	0.660

The information in Table 7.3 suggests that Model D is the best one, with the smallest mean and S.E.

In the navigation tree for text output, click "Model Fit", and you will find the AIC table (Table 7.4).

Table 7.4 Fit measures (AIC)

Models	AIC	BCC	BIC	CAIC
A	20.000	24.167	34.012	44.012
B	18.506	22.256	31.117	40.117
C	19.924	23.674	32.535	41.535
D	18.319	21.652	29.528	37.528
E	20.729	24.479	33.340	42.340

The fit measures in Table 7.4 further support that Model D is the best one. In other words, compared with other models, Model D is the most optimal. This is because it has the smallest AIC, BCC, BIC, and CAIC values, as well as the smallest mean ML discrepancy. Bootstrap can also be used to compare non-nested models. When non-nested models are compared, the separated analysis should be performed to calculate the mean discrepancy and the fit measures.

7.2 Bootstrapping Used in Estimation Method Comparison

Bootstrapping can be used in estimation method comparison. To perform the comparison, the bootstrap program uses the ADF, ML, GLS or ULS discrepancy to fit a specific model to the bootstrap samples to examine how well the model fits the samples. It measures the discrepancies between the population and the implied moments of the samples using x^2_{ADF}, x^2_{ML}, x^2_{GLS}, and x^2_{ULS} [to examine the difference between the implied bootstrap sample moments and the population (original sample) moments]. The estimation method which produces the smallest discrepancy means across all measures is considered to be the best method.

7.2.1 Dataset and Task

Now we will use the data displayed in Table 7.1 to compare different estimation methods for the following model (Figure 7.9). The methods include ADF, ML, GLS, and ULS.

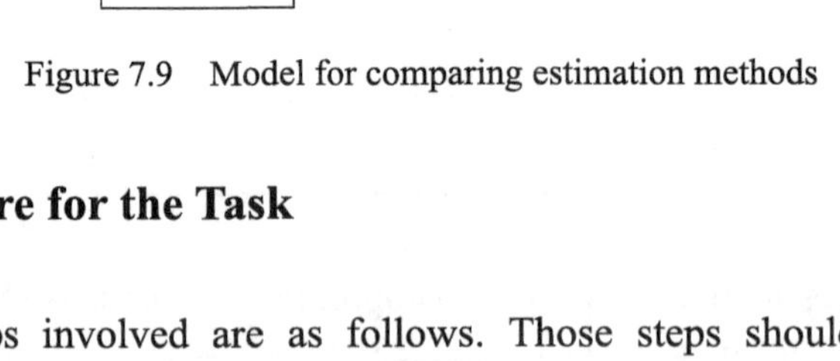

Figure 7.9 Model for comparing estimation methods

7.2.2 Procedure for the Task

The key steps involved are as follows. Those steps should be followed for evaluating each of the four estimation methods.

Now let's begin with the assessment of ADF. Import the data file. Draw a path diagram like Figure 7.9. Fix the regressions of SSE on FTT and STT at 0. Right-click each arrow, and open the "Object Properties" dialogue box; click the "Parameters" tab; enter "0" in the "Regression weight" text box. Click the "Estimation" tab, and select "Asymptotically distribution-free" (Figure 7.10).

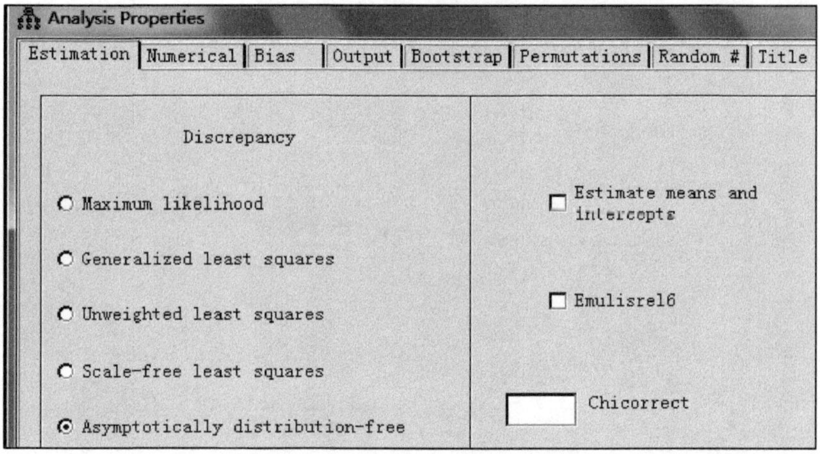

Figure 7.10 Requesting estimation by an asymptotically distribution-free criterion

In the "Analysis Properties" dialogue box, click the "Random #" tab. Select an arbitrary seed value. Here "1" is selected. Use the same seed for every analysis later (Figure 7.11).

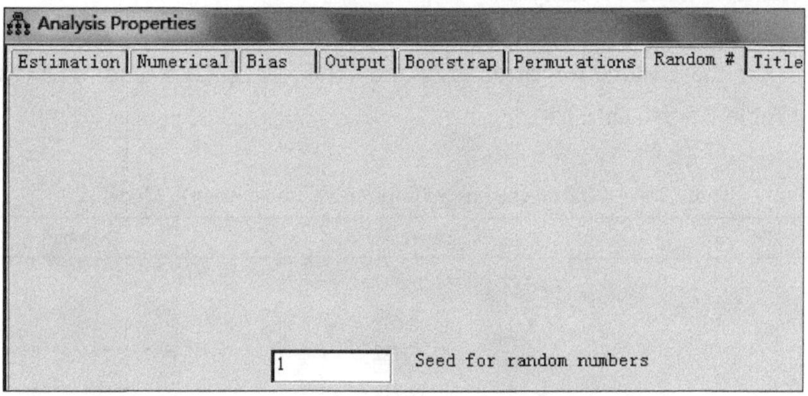

Figure 7.11 Setting the seed for random numbers

Click the "Bootstrap" tab, and type "1,000" in the "Number of bootstrap samples" text box. Select the "Bootstrap ADF" "Bootstrap ML" "Bootstrap GLS" "Bootstrap ULS", which suggests that x_{ADF}^2, x_{ML}^2, x_{GLS}^2 and x_{ULS}^2 are to be employed to examine the discrepancy between the original sample moments and each of the implied moments of the bootstrap samples (Figure 7.12). Close the dialogue box and we can run the analysis.

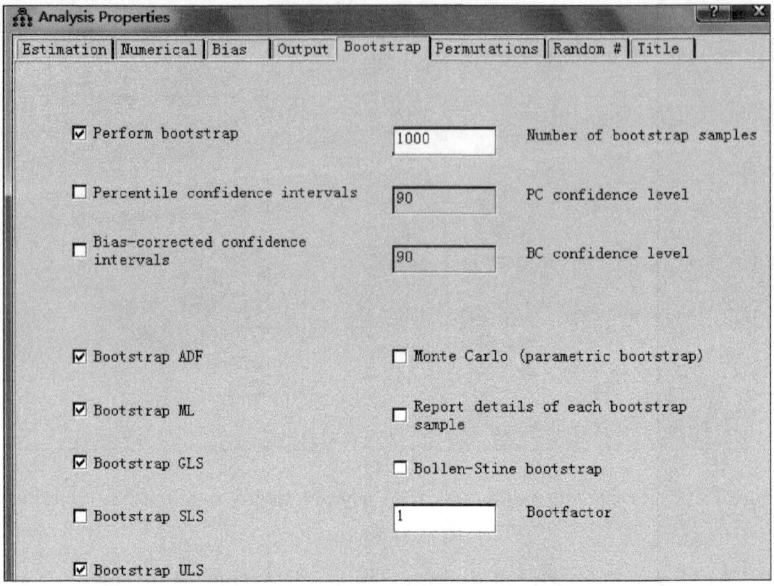

Figure 7.12　Specify the bootstrap options

7.2.3　Results of the Analysis

Here are the results for evaluating the ADF, ML, GLS and ULS estimation methods (Table 7.5 to Table 7.8).

Table 7.5　ADF discrepancy (implied vs. population) (Model A)

Summary	Discrepancy	Distribution
	…	…
	3.931	|***
	7.822	|******************
	11.712	|*******************
	15.603	|*********************
	19.493	|*************
N = 1,000 Mean = 15.945 S.E. = 0.249	23.384	|*********
	27.274	|****
	31.165	|**
	35.055	|*
	38.946	|*
	42.836	|*
	46.727	|*

Continued

Summary	Discrepancy	Distribution
	50.617	|*
N = 1,000 Mean = 15.945 S.E. = 0.249	54.508	|*
	58.398	|*
	…	…

Table 7.6 ML discrepancy (implied vs. population) (Model A)

Summary	Discrepancy	Distribution
	…	…
	–3,002.475	|*
	185.273	|********************
	3,373.021	|*
	6,560.769	|
	9,748.517	|
	12,936.265	|
	16,124.014	|*
N = 1,000 Mean = 126.398 S.E. = 47.129	19,311.762	|
	22,499.510	|
	25,687.258	|
	28,875.006	|
	32,062.754	|
	35,250.502	|
	38,438.250	|
	41,625.998	|*
	…	…

Table 7.7 GLS discrepancy (implied vs. population) (Model A)

Summary	Discrepancy	Distribution
	…	…
	3.121	|*****
	7.557	|********************
N = 1,000 Mean = 13.752 S.E. = 0.245	11.992	|*******************
	16.428	|***********
	20.863	|*******
	25.298	|****
	29.734	|**

Continued

Summary	Discrepancy	Distribution
	34.169	|*
	38.605	|*
	43.040	|*
	47.476	|*
N = 1,000 Mean = 13.752 S.E. = 0.245	51.911	|
	56.347	|
	60.782	|
	65.218	|*
	…	…

Table 7.8 ULS discrepancy (implied vs. population) (Model A)

Summary	Discrepancy	Distribution
	…	…
	469.077	|*******************
	38,689.062	|***************
	76,909.048	|********
	115,129.033	|*****
	153,349.018	|***
	191,569.003	|*
	229,788.989	|*
N = 1,000 Mean = 54,499.394 S.E. = 2,107.728	268,008.974	|*
	306,228.959	|*
	344,448.944	|*
	382,668.929	|*
	420,888.915	|*
	459,108.900	|*
	497,328.885	|*
	535,548.870	|
	…	…

In similar ways, we can obtain the results for evaluating the estimation methods (details are omitted).

Table 7.9 is a summary of the results from evaluating each of the estimation methods. The results suggest that ML is the best method (with the smallest discrepancy in three of the four columns).

Table 7.9 Summary of results from evaluating the estimation methods

Methods	x^2_{ADF}	x^2_{ML}	x^2_{GLS}	x^2_{ULS}
ADF	15.945 (0.249)	126.398 (47.129)	13.752 (0.245)	54,499.394 (2,107.728)
ML	15.686 (0.226)	21.071 (0.580)	10.696 (0.177)	34,453.221 (1,248.859)
GLS	16.828 (0.278)	31.885 (0.887)	10.376 (0.153)	36,252.899 (1,274.090)
ULS	21.039 (0.382)	22.261 (0.647)	14.178 (0.268)	34,466.319 (1,248.993)

7.3 Summary

As a technique to produce new samples from the original sample, bootstrapping can be employed to compare the fit of competing models and the appropriateness of alternative estimation methods. To compare competing models, we have to analyze each model separately. In the "Analysis Properties" window, we have to specify our task, decide the number of samples to be produced, choose the random seed to be used, and set the convergence criteria as well as the iteration limit. When examining the results, we must ensure that all the produced samples are used in the analysis. In case that *n* samples are unused for a particular model, we have to repeat the analysis with more than *n* samples to be produced in the property setting. The model with the smallest AIC, BCC, BIC, CAIC and mean ML discrepancy values is the most preferable. When comparing the estimation methods, we have to check the methods to be compared, select the same random seed and the number of samples to be bootstrapped for each analysis, and specify the discrepancy function corresponding to each estimation method. The method with the smallest values on all or most of the discrepancy functions is the best.

References

Arbuckle, J. L. 2006. Amos 7.0 User's Guide. http://www.hsc.edu.kw/student/app_manuals/SPSS/Amos%207.0%20User%27s%20Guide.pdf [2018-6-6].

Baker, D. L., Stoolmiller, M., Good III, R. H., et al. 2011. Effect of reading comprehension on passage fluency in Spanish and English for second-grade English learners. *School Psychology Review*, 40(3): 331-351.

Byrne, B. M. 2010. *Structural Equation Modeling with AMOS*: *Basic Concepts*, *Applications*, *and Programming*. 2nd edn. New York: Taylor & Francis Group.

Davies, A. & Elder, C. 2004. *The Handbook of Applied Linguistics*. Malden: Blackwell Publishing Ltd.

Guo, Y. & Roehrig, A. D. 2011. Roles of general versus second language (L2) knowledge in L2 reading comprehension. *Reading in a Foreign Language*, 23(1): 42-64.

Kline, R. B. 2011. *Principles and Practice of Structural Equation Modeling*. 3rd edn. New York: The Guilford Press.

Laney, D. 2001. 3-D data management: Controlling data volume, velocity, and variety. https://blogs.gartner.com/doug-laney/files/2012/01/ad949-3D-Data-Management-Controlling-Data-Volume-Velocity- and-Variety.pdf [2018-6-6].

Laney, D. 2012. Deja VVVu: Others claiming Gartner's construct for big data. https://blogs.gartner.com/doug-laney/deja-vvvue-others-claiming-gartners-volume-velocity-variety-construct-for-big-data/ [2018-6-6].

Lin, M. H. 2016. Effects of corpus-aided language learning in the EFL grammar classroom: A case study of students' learning attitudes and teachers' perceptions in Taiwan. *TESOL Quarterly*, 50(4): 871-893.

Liu, D. & Jiang, P. 2009. Using a corpus-based lexicogrammatical approach to grammar instruction in EFL and ESL contexts. *The Modern Language Journal*, 93(1): 61-78.

Lu, X. F. 2011. A corpus-based evaluation of syntactic complexity measures as indices of college-level ESL writers's language development. *TESOL Quarterly*, 45(1): 36-62.

Lu, X. F. 2012. The relationship of lexical richness to the quality of ESL learners' oral narratives. *The Modern Language Journal*, 96(2): 190-208.

Lu, X. F. & Ai, H. Y. 2015. Syntactic complexity in college-level English writing: Differences among writers with diverse L1 backgrounds. *Journal of Second Language Writing*, (29): 16-27.

Netten, A., Droop, M. & Verhoeven, L. 2011. Predictors of reading literacy for first and second language learners. *Reading and Writing*, 24(4): 413-425.

Phoocharoensil, S. 2012. Language corpora for EFL teachers: An exploration of English grammar through concordance lines. *Procedia-Social and Behavioral Sciences*, (64): 507-514.

Pulido, D. & Hambrick, D. Z. 2008. The virtuous circle: Modeling individual differences in L2 reading and vocabulary development. *Reading in a Foreign Language*, 20(2): 164-190.

Raykov, T. & Marcoulides, G. A. 2006. *A First Course in Structural Equation Modeling.* 2nd edn. Mahwah: Lawrence Erlbaum Associates, Inc., Publishers.

Verhoeven, L. & Leeuwe, J. V. 2012. The simple view of second language reading throughout the primary grades. *Reading & Writing*, 25(8): 1805-1818.

Wu, W. C. V., Yen, L. L. & Marek, M. 2011. Using online EFL interaction to increase confidence, motivation, and ability. *Journal of Educational Technology & Society*, 14(3): 118-129.

Zhang, D. B. 2012. Vocabulary and grammar knowledge in second language reading comprehension: A structural equation modeling study. *The Modern Language Journal*, 96(4): 558-575.